Crochet

Patterns, Tips and Techniques

Consulting by Heidi Beazley

Written by Beth Taylor

Photo styling by Ewelina Rusek and Amy Stark

Photography by Christopher Hiltz
Additional photography from Getty and Shutterstock.com

Crochet symbols and abbreviations from Craft Yarn Council's www.YarnStandards.com

Copyright © 2024 Publications International, Ltd. All rights reserved.
This book may not be reproduced or quoted in whole or in part
by any means whatsoever without written permission from:

Louis Weber, CEO
Publications International, Ltd.
8140 Lehigh Avenue
Morton Grove, IL 60053

Permission is never granted for commercial purposes.

ISBN: 978-1-63938-684-0

Manufactured in China.

8 7 6 5 4 3 2 1

Publications International, Ltd.

Contents

What You'll Need

Crochet Hooks

Crochet hooks can be made from aluminum, plastic, wood, or bamboo. They are available in a wide range of sizes and are used with an assortment of yarns. Steel hooks are the smallest and are often used with fine thread in delicate crochet work, such as lace and doilies. Most patterns and yarn labels recommend a hook size. Select a crochet hook that feels comfortable to you and works well with your project and yarn.

Common Hook Sizes

U.S.	B-1	C-2	D-3	E-4	F-5	G-6	7	H-8	I-9	J-10	K-10.5	L-11	M-13	N-15	P	Q	S
mm	2.25	2.75	3.25	3.5	3.75	4	4.5	5	5.5	6	6.5	8	9	10	15	16	19

Needles

Tapestry or yarn needles have a blunt tip and an eye large enough to accommodate thick yarns. These special needles can be used to weave in yarn tails or sew crocheted pieces together.

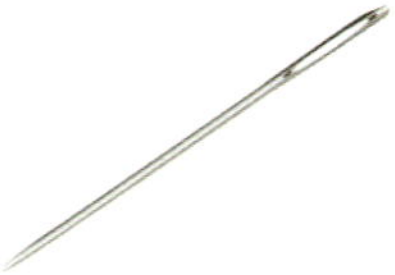

Stitch Markers

As their name suggests, stitch markers are designed to mark your stitches. They can be used to mark a certain number of stitches, the beginning of a round, or where to make a particular stitch. Stitch markers must have openings so that they can be easily removed. You can purchase stitch markers, or improvise with pins, earrings, or safety pins.

Pins

Use long, rustproof pins for blocking and pinning seams together. Pins can also serve as stitch markers. Opt for pins with large, colorful heads that won't get lost in your crochet work.

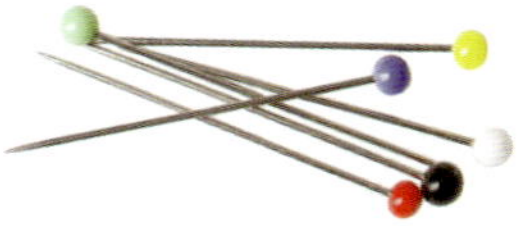

Measurement Tools

Measuring tape is a must-have tool when taking body measurements before making garments. Measuring tape and rulers can be used to measure gauge.

All About Yarn

Yarn for Beginners

Before starting any new crochet project, you must select your yarn. For beginners learning the basic stitches, select a simple cotton yarn that is light colored, smooth, and sturdy. It's harder to see your stitches with dark colored yarn. Avoid fuzzy and loosely woven yarns that fray easily.

Yarn Fibers

Natural fibers

Cotton, linen, and hemp yarns are made from plant fibers. They are lightweight, breathable, and machine washable. Mercerized cotton has undergone a chemical process that results in stronger, shinier yarn.

Yarns made from animal fibers include wool, silk, cashmere, mohair, alpaca, and angora. These animal fibers are much warmer than plant fibers. Both types of natural fibers offer a bit of stretch.

Synthetic fibers

Yarns made from synthetic fibers include nylon, rayon, acrylic, and polyester. Synthetic yarns are usually less expensive than natural fibers, but are less breathable and pill more easily.

Novelty and specialty yarns

Novelty and specialty yarns can be tricky to work with, but create a distinctive look. They include bouclé, ladder, eyelash, and chenille. While great for trims and accessories, novelty yarn is not best for beginners.

Selecting Your Yarn

Each package of store-bought yarn has a label listing the yarn's length, fiber content, and weight. Yarn weight refers to the thickness of a yarn. It ranges from the thinnest embroidery thread to the bulkiest yarn. Yarn labels also recommend hook size—just look for the crochet hook symbol to find the U.S. and metric hook size.

Yarn Weight Guidelines

LACE 0

Yarn types: Fingering, lace, and 10-count crochet thread
Recommended hook sizes (metric): 1.5–2.25 mm
Recommended hook sizes (U.S.): Steel 6 to B-1
Crochet gauge range: 32–42 double crochet stitches to 4 in.

SUPER FINE 1

Yarn types: Sock, fingering, and baby
Recommended hook sizes (metric): 2.25–3.5 mm
Recommended hook sizes (U.S.): B-1 to E-4
Crochet gauge range: 21–32 single crochet stitches to 4 in.

FINE 2

Yarn types: Sport and baby
Recommended hook sizes (metric): 3.5–4.5 mm
Recommended hook sizes (U.S.): E-4 to 7
Crochet gauge range: 16–20 single crochet stitches to 4 in.

LIGHT 3

Yarn types: Double knitting and light worsted
Recommended hook sizes (metric): 4.5–5.5 mm
Recommended hook sizes (U.S.): 7 to I-9
Crochet gauge range: 12–17 single crochet stitches to 4 in.

MEDIUM 4

Yarn types: Afghan, aran, and worsted
Recommended hook sizes (metric): 5.5–6.5 mm
Recommended hook sizes (U.S.): I-9 to K-10.5
Crochet gauge range: 11–14 single crochet stitches to 4 in.

BULKY 5

Yarn types: Chunky, craft, and rug
Recommended hook sizes (metric): 6.5–9 mm
Recommended hook sizes (U.S.): K-10.5 to M-13
Crochet gauge range: 8–11 single crochet stitches to 4 in.

SUPER BULKY 6

Yarn types: Bulky and roving
Recommended hook sizes (metric): 9–15 mm
Recommended hook sizes (U.S.): M-13 to Q
Crochet gauge range: 7–9 single crochet stitches to 4 in.

JUMBO 7

Yarn types: Jumbo and roving
Recommended hook sizes (metric): 15 mm and larger
Recommended hook sizes (U.S.): Q and larger
Crochet gauge range: 6 single crochet stitches and fewer to 4 in.

Source: Craft Yarn Council's www.YarnStandards.com

Holding the Hook

Pencil Hold

Knife Hold

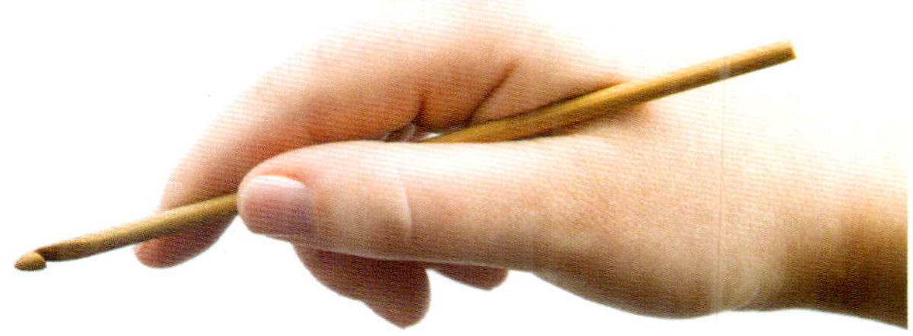

Tip: The instructions and photographs in this book are intended for right-handed crocheters. If you are a lefty, try holding up a mirror to the edge of a photograph to see the left-handed version.

Holding the Yarn

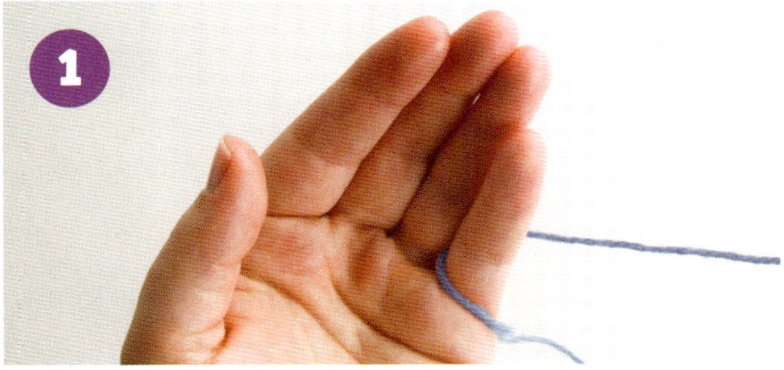

With your palm facing up, weave the working yarn (the yarn coming from the ball) between your pinky and ring fingers. Wrap the yarn clockwise around your pinky.

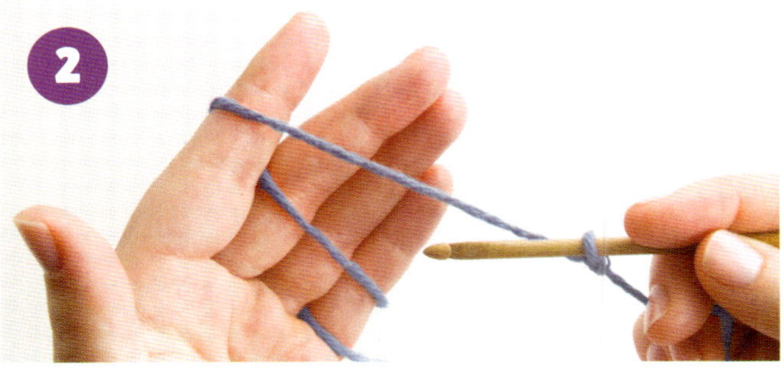

Take the yarn across your ring and middle fingers. Then wrap the yarn under and around your index finger.

Hold the yarn under the slip knot with your left thumb and middle finger.

Tip: There are many ways to hold your yarn. Experiment with different methods until you find what is most comfortable for you.

Making a Slip Knot

The first step in any crochet project is a slip knot. The slip knot is what attaches the yarn to your hook.

Wrap the yarn around your index and middle fingers on your yarn hand to create an X.

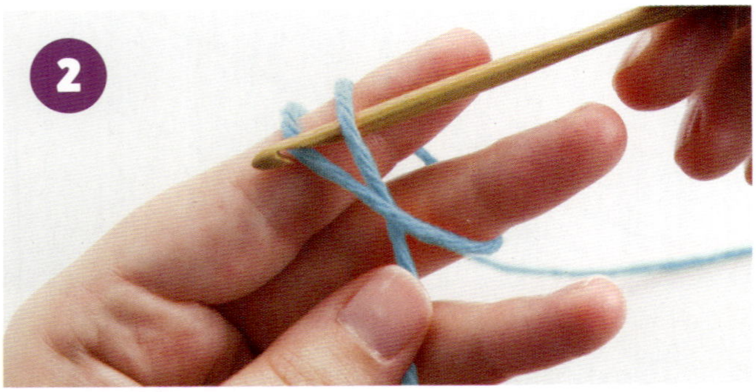

From the top, insert your hook under the first loop to grab the second loop.

Draw the second loop you just grabbed under and up through the first loop.

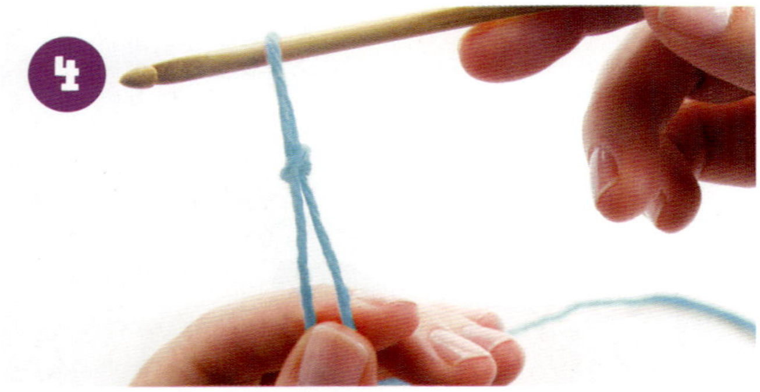

Slide your fingers out. Pull your hook up while gently pulling both ends of the yarn down.

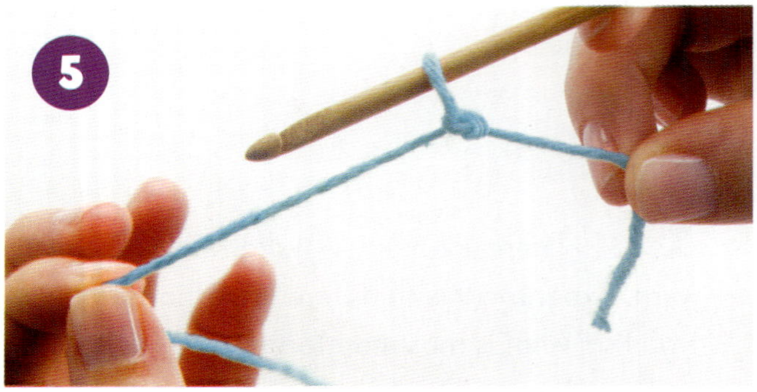

Pull the ends of the yarn to tighten the slip knot close to your hook.

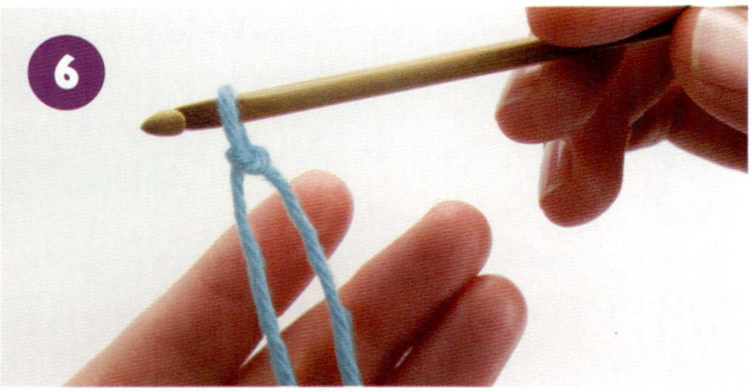

With a finished slip knot around your hook, you are ready to start crocheting.

Chain Stitch (ch)

Crochet often begins with a series of chain stitches used to make up the first row. This is called the foundation chain and is the basic start to most crochet projects.

Start with a slip knot on your hook. Hold the yarn tail for tension.

Bring the working yarn (the yarn coming from the ball) over your hook from back to front. This is called yarn over (yo).

Draw this section of yarn back through the slip knot. You will have 1 new loop on your hook when your first chain stitch is complete.

Yarn over again.

Draw this section of yarn through the loop on your hook. You will have 1 new loop on your hook each time you complete a chain stitch.

Repeat steps 4–5 until your foundation chain has the required number of chain stitches.

Counting Chains

Crochet patterns usually begin by telling you the number of chains needed for the foundation chain.

Identifying the Front and Back

The front of the foundation chain looks like a braid with a series of Vs. The back side of the foundation chain has a vertical ridge of bumps running down the middle from your hook to the end of the chain. Count chains from the front side.

Counting

Begin counting from the top of the foundation chain. Do not count the loop on your hook or the slip knot on the bottom. Count only completed, V-shaped chain stitches. This example has 13 completed chain stitches.

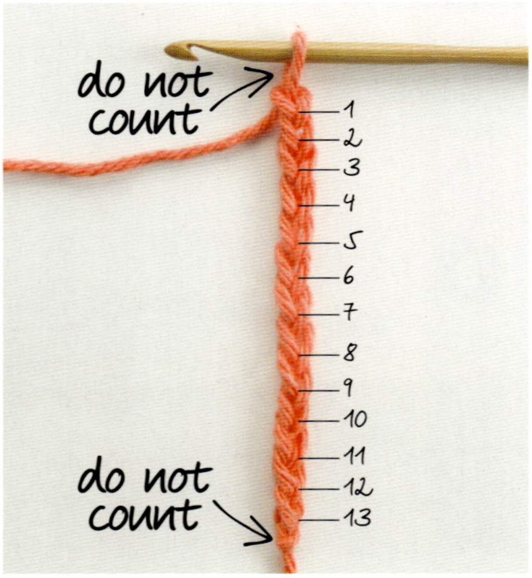

Tip: When creating a long foundation chain, it is helpful to use stitch markers every 10 or 20 stitches to make counting easier.

Turning Chains (tch)

Stitch	Number of Turning Chains
Slip stitch	0
Single crochet	1
Half double crochet	2
Double crochet	3
Treble crochet	4

Each crochet stitch requires a specific number of turning chains at the beginning or end of a row. The number of extra stitches needed for the turning chain is added to the number needed for the foundation chain.

Tension

Tension keeps your stitches neat and consistent. Make sure the chains in your foundation chain are even and loose enough to allow your hook back into those chains for the next row.

Too loose

Too tight

Just right

Slip Stitch (sl st)

The slip stitch is one of the most basic crochet stitches and is often used for joining.

Start with a foundation chain on your hook. Insert your hook from front to back into the second chain from your hook. There are 2 loops on your hook.

Yarn over, bringing the working yarn over your hook from back to front.

Draw the yarn through both loops on your hook. You will have 1 new loop on your hook when your first slip stitch is complete.

Single Crochet (sc)

How to single crochet:

To begin a row of single crochet, first stitch a foundation chain to the desired length. Add 1 extra chain stitch for the turning chain.

Insert your hook from front to back into the second chain stitch from your hook. There will now be 2 loops on your hook.

Yarn over. Draw this yarn through the first loop on your hook. There will be 2 loops on your hook.

Yarn over again and draw this yarn through both loops on your hook. You will have 1 loop remaining on your hook when your first single crochet is complete.

Insert your hook into the next chain stitch. Repeat steps 2–3 to complete another single crochet stitch.

Repeat step 4, working a single crochet stitch into each chain. At the end of the row, make 1 chain stitch for the turning chain.

Turn your work so that the opposite side faces you. Insert your hook into the first single crochet stitch of the previous row and repeat steps 2–3. (Skip the turning chain.)

Insert your hook into the next stitch and repeat steps 2–3, working a single crochet stitch into each single crochet of the previous row.

Repeat step 7 to continue the pattern. At the end of this and all subsequent rows, chain 1 for the turning chain and turn your work.

Half Double Crochet (hdc)

How to half double crochet:

To begin a row of half double crochet, first stitch a foundation chain to the desired length. Add 2 extra chain stitches for the turning chain.

Yarn over. With this yarn over, insert your hook into the third chain stitch from your hook. There will be 3 loops on your hook.

Yarn over again. Draw the yarn through the first loop only. There will still be 3 loops on your hook.

Yarn over and draw the yarn through all 3 loops on your hook.

You will have 1 loop on your hook when your first half double crochet is complete.

Yarn over. With this yarn over, insert your hook into the next chain stitch. There will be 3 loops on your hook. Repeat steps 2–4 to complete another half double crochet stitch.

Repeat step 5, working a half double crochet stitch into each chain stitch. At the end of the row, chain 2 for the turning chain.

Turn your work so that the opposite side faces you. Yarn over and insert your hook into the second stitch. (The turning chain counts as the first half double crochet stitch in this row.) Repeat steps 2–4 to complete the half double crochet stitch.

Repeat step 5 to continue making half double crochet stitches into each stitch of the previous row. At the end of this and all subsequent rows, chain 2 for the turning chain and turn.

Double Crochet (dc)

How to double crochet:

To begin a row of double crochet, first stitch a foundation chain to the desired length. Add 3 extra chain stitches for the turning chain.

Yarn over. With this yarn over, insert your hook into the fourth chain stitch from your hook. There will be 3 loops on your hook.

Yarn over. Draw the yarn through the first loop on your hook. There will be 3 loops on your hook.

Yarn over. Draw the yarn through the first 2 loops on your hook only. There will now be 2 loops on your hook.

Yarn over again. Draw the yarn through the remaining 2 loops on your hook. You will have 1 loop on your hook when your first double crochet is complete.

Yarn over. Insert your hook into the next chain stitch. Repeat steps 2–4 to complete another double crochet stitch.

Repeat step 5, working a double crochet stitch into each chain stitch. At the end of the row, chain 3 for the turning chain. Turn your work so that the opposite side faces you.

Yarn over and insert your hook into the second stitch. (The turning chain counts as the first double crochet stitch in this row.) Repeat steps 2–4 to complete the double crochet stitch.

Repeat step 5 to continue making double crochet stitches into each stitch of the previous row. At the end of this and all subsequent rows, chain 3 for the turning chain and turn.

Treble Crochet (tr)

How to treble crochet:

To begin a row of treble crochet, first stitch a foundation chain to the desired length. Add 4 extra chain stitches for the turning chain.

Yarn over twice. Insert your hook into the fifth chain stitch from your hook. There will now be 4 loops on your hook.

Yarn over once. Draw the yarn through the first loop on your hook. There will be 4 loops on your hook.

Yarn over once. Draw the yarn through the first 2 loops on your hook. There will be 3 loops on your hook.

Yarn over once. Draw the yarn through the first 2 loops on your hook again. There will be 2 loops on your hook.

Yarn over once. Draw the yarn through the remaining 2 loops on your hook. You will have 1 loop on your hook when your first treble crochet is complete.

Yarn over twice and insert your hook into the next chain stitch. Repeat steps 2–5 to complete another treble crochet stitch.

Repeat step 6, working a treble crochet stitch into each chain. At the end of the row, chain 4 for the turning chain. Turn your work so that the opposite side faces you. Yarn over twice and insert your hook into the second stitch. Repeat steps 2–5 to complete the treble crochet stitch.

Repeat step 6 to continue making treble crochet stitches into each stitch of the previous row. At the end of this and all subsequent rows, chain 4 for the turning chain and turn.

Decreasing Stitches (dec)

To decrease within a row, combine multiple stitches together.

Single Crochet 2 Together (sc2tog)

Insert your hook into the next stitch as you would to start a single crochet.

Yarn over and draw the yarn through the stitch. There are now 2 loops on your hook.

Insert your hook into the next stitch. Yarn over and draw the yarn through the stitch. There are 3 loops on your hook.

Yarn over and draw the yarn through all 3 loops on your hook. You will have 1 loop on your hook when your first single crochet 2 together (sc2tog) is complete.

Double Crochet 2 Together (dc2tog)

Yarn over and insert hook into next stitch. Yarn over and draw yarn through stitch. Yarn over and draw yarn through first 2 loops. You will have 2 loops on hook.

Yarn over and insert hook into next stitch. Yarn over and draw yarn through stitch. Yarn over and draw yarn through first 2 loops. You will have 3 loops on hook.

Yarn over and draw the yarn through all 3 loops on your hook. You will have 1 loop on your hook when your first double crochet 2 together (dc2tog) is complete.

Increasing Stitches (inc)

To increase within a row, work multiple stitches into the same stitch.

Single Crochet Increase (sc inc)

Insert your hook back into the same stitch you did your last single crochet in. Work another single crochet into that same stitch.

You will have 1 loop on your hook when your first single crochet increase is complete.

Double Crochet Increase (dc inc)

Insert your hook back into the same stitch in the previous row. Work another double crochet into that same stitch.

You will have 1 loop on your hook when your first double crochet increase is complete.

Front & Back Loops (FL & BL)

Working into the front or back loop only will create a unique texture and line. These examples use half double crochet, but you can use these techniques with other stitches.

Tip: When your crochet work is in front of you, the front loop is the loop closer to you, while the back loop is farther from you.

Front Loops

To work a half double crochet stitch into the front loop only (or flo), yarn over and insert your hook into only the front loop closer to you. Complete the stitch as usual.

Continue working half double crochet stitches into only the front loops of the stitches in the previous row until you reach the end of the row. This creates a line.

Back Loops

To work a half double crochet stitch into the back loop only (or blo), yarn over and insert your hook into only the back loop farther from you. Complete the stitch as usual.

Continue working half double crochet stitches into only the back loops of the stitches in the previous row until you reach the end of the row. This creates another line.

Working into Spaces

Some patterns will ask you to work into a space rather than a stitch of a previous row or round. This technique is demonstrated below using double crochet, but you can use other stitches.

Start at the position where you want to work into a space. Yarn over.

Insert your hook from front to back into the space (instead of the stitch). Yarn over and draw the yarn through the space.

Finish your double crochet as usual. You will have 1 loop on your hook when your first double crochet stitch into the space is complete.

Here is the row finished with double crochet stitches worked into the spaces.

Tip: Working into spaces is often called for when starting a round and in many floral motifs. In the example to the right, multiple stitches have been made into the spaces.

Working in Rounds

To begin working in rounds, you have to first start with a center ring.
There are 2 different methods for starting a round: with a chain stitch ring or a magic circle.

Chain Stitch Ring

The chain stitch ring is made up of chain stitches that are joined together to form a ring. This method leaves a small opening in the center of your round.

Tip: Patterns will tell you how many chains to start with and what stitches to use. This example uses single crochet.

Chain 5 for a foundation chain. Insert your hook back into the first chain you made.

Work a slip stitch into that chain to form a ring.

Insert your hook into the center of the ring. Work a single crochet stitch into the ring.

Continue working single crochet stitches into the ring until you have made the required number of stitches. (For this example, 6 single crochet stitches.)

Work a slip stitch into the first single crochet you made to close up the ring.

You are now ready to start a round.
(See page 27.)

Magic Circle

The magic circle forms a ring with your yarn to which your first round of stitches are attached. The ends are pulled to leave no opening in the center. That's the magic!

Tip: A chain stitch ring can replace a magic circle in a pattern.

Loop the yarn around your fingers as shown to form an X.

Take your hook under the bottom strand of the X. Use your hook to draw the other strand under the bottom strand. It will form a loose loop on your hook.

Remove the circle of yarn from your fingers. Yarn over. Draw the yarn through the loop on your hook. (This does not count as your first single crochet stitch.)

With your magic circle complete, you should now have a circle with the tail and the working yarn on the left side.

Insert your hook into the center of the circle. You are going to work a single crochet into that space. Yarn over and draw the yarn through the circle and tail. You will have 2 loops on your hook.

Yarn over again and draw the yarn through the remaining 2 loops on your hook. You will have 1 loop on your hook when your first single crochet stitch into the circle is complete.

Continue working the required number of single crochet stitches into the circle, making sure you are always working around the circle and the tail. If you run out of tail, pull it slightly. This closes the circle a little, but allows you to have a longer tail to work around.

When you have worked 6 single crochet stitches into the circle, pull the tail tightly to close the circle.

Insert your hook into the first single crochet stitch you made and make a slip stitch to close the circle.

With your slip stitch complete, you are now ready to start a round.

Starting a Round

To start a round, first begin by using either the chain stitch ring or magic circle method. This example used the magic circle method.

Round 1:

Chain 1. Insert your hook under the top 2 loops of the first stitch and work a single crochet into that stitch.

Work 2 single crochets into each of the remaining stitches. (You will have 12 stitches.) Insert your hook back into the first stitch and make a slip stitch to close the round.

Rounds 2-6:

Each round increases by 6 stitches. The increases are evenly spaced in order to keep the circular shape. Close each round with a slip stitch back into the first stitch and then chain 1.

Round 2: Single crochet an increase in every other stitch for a total of 18 stitches.

Round 3: Single crochet an increase in every third stitch for a total of 24 stitches.

Round 4: Single crochet an increase in every fourth stitch for a total of 30 stitches.

Round 5: Single crochet an increase in every fifth stitch for a total of 36 stitches.

Round 6: Single crochet an increase in every sixth stitch for a total of 42 stitches.

For additional rounds, continue to evenly increase your rounds by 6 until your desired circumference.

Joining in New Yarn

At the End of a Row

To join in new yarn at the end of a row, work the last stitch with the old yarn until the final yarn over of the stitch. Yarn over with the new yarn.

Draw the new yarn through both loops on your hook. There is 1 loop on your hook. Continue stitching with the new yarn as usual.

In the Middle of a Row

To join in new yarn in the middle of a row, work the last stitch with the old yarn until the final yarn over of the stitch. Yarn over with the new yarn.

Draw the new yarn through both loops on your hook. There is 1 loop on your hook. Continue stitching with the new yarn as usual until you reach the end of the row.

Tip: Rather than leaving the tail of the old yarn in the middle of the row, you can work over the old yarn until you reach the end of the row. You can then weave in all yarn tails at the edges later.

Fastening Off

After completing your last stitch, cut the excess yarn, leaving several inches to weave the tail in later. Yarn over and draw the yarn tail through the loop on your hook.

Pull the yarn tail to tighten.

Weaving in the Tail

Thread one of your yarn tails into a blunt-tipped tapestry needle. Insert the needle into the first stitch and draw the yarn through.

Continue weaving the needle under and over the stitches around the edge.

Cut the yarn close to the final stitch when you're done weaving in the tail.

Crossed Stitches

Crossed stitches cross back over the front of previous stitches to form a unique X pattern. Double and treble crochet are the most common stitches used to cross.

To make crossed stitches using double crochet, start with a foundation chain that has a multiple of 2 chains.

Row 1:

1

In the fifth chain from your hook, work 1 double crochet. There is 1 loop on your hook.

2

Crossing over the front of the double crochet stitch you just made, work 1 double crochet into the last skipped chain.

3

You will have 1 loop on your hook when your first pair of crossed stitches is complete.

4

Chain 1. Skip 1 chain and work 1 double crochet into the next chain after that.

Crossing over the front of the double crochet stitch you just made, work 1 double crochet into the last skipped chain.

Repeat steps 4–5 across the row. At the end of the row, work 1 double crochet into the last chain.

Chain 3 for the turning chain. Turn your work so that the opposite side faces you.

Tip: How to make crossed treble stitches:

1. Start with an odd number foundation chain.
2. In the sixth chain from your hook, work 1 treble crochet stitch.
3. Follow steps 2–6, replacing double crochet with treble crochet stitches.
4. Chain 4 for the turning chain and turn.

Row 2:

1. Skip the first 2 stitches and work 1 double crochet into the next double crochet stitch.
2. Crossing over the front of the double crochet you just made, work 1 double crochet into the last skipped stitch.
3. Chain 1. Skip the next double crochet stitch and work 1 double crochet into the last skipped stitch.
4. Repeat step 3 until the last stitch of the row. Work 1 double crochet into the last stitch.
5. Chain 3 and turn.

Repeat row 2 to continue the pattern.

Popcorns (pc)

The popcorn stitch works several stitches into the same space, resulting in a "puffed" pattern and texture.

To make a popcorn using single and double crochet, start with a foundation chain that has a multiple of 3 chain stitches.

Row 1:

Work 1 single crochet into the second chain from your hook.

Finish the row with single crochet stitches. Chain 1 for the turning chain.

Row 2:

Turn your work so the opposite side faces you. Work a single crochet into each of the next 2 stitches.

In the next stitch, work 5 double crochets into the same stitch. Drop the loop you created by removing your hook.

Insert your hook under the top 2 loops of the first double crochet of the group.

Grab the dropped loop with your hook and draw the yarn through the stitch. Add a chain stitch to complete your first popcorn stitch. You will have 1 loop on your hook.

Work 1 single crochet into each of the next 3 stitches.

Continue to the end of the row, alternating between the popcorn stitch and the single crochet stitches. At the end of row, chain 1 for the turning chain.

Row 3:

Turn your work so the opposite side faces you. Work 1 single crochet stitch into each stitch across the row.

Repeat rows 2–3 to continue the pattern.

Tip: For rows of staggered popcorn stitches like in our example swatch, reduce the number of single crochet stitches at the beginning of every other popcorn row. Then complete the popcorn rows as usual.

V-Stitch

The V-stitch makes a series of interlocking Vs. This stitch works up quickly and is great for making afghans.

To make V-stitches using double crochet, start with a foundation chain that has a multiple of 3 chains, plus 7.

Row 1:

Work 1 double crochet into the fourth chain from your hook. Chain 1.

Skip 1 chain stitch and work 1 double crochet into the next chain. Chain 1.

Work 1 double crochet into the very same chain. You will have 1 loop on your hook when your first V-stitch is complete.

Skip 2 chains and work 1 double crochet into the next chain. Chain 1. Work 1 double crochet into the very same stitch.

Repeat step 4 across the row until you have 4 chains left. Chain 1.

Skip 2 chains. Work 1 double crochet into each of the last 2 chains to end the row.

At the end of the row, chain 3 for the turning chain. Turn your work so the opposite side faces you.

Tip: A chain-1 space is the space created by the chain 1 between the 2 double crochet stitches. It looks like the center of a V.

Row 2:

The turning chain counts as the first double crochet in this row. Work 1 double crochet into the next stitch and chain 1.

Work 1 V-stitch into each chain-1 space (center of each V) across the row until you have 1 chain space and 2 double crochet stitches left.

3 When you have 1 chain space and 2 double crochet stitches left, chain 1 and skip the chain-1 space. Work 1 double crochet into each of the last 2 double crochet stitches to end the row. Chain 3 for the turning chain and turn.

Repeat row 2 to continue the pattern.

Chevrons

A chevron is a classic stitch pattern that is great for baby blankets. Try alternating colors to accentuate the pattern. This example works 3 double crochets into 1 stitch to create the points.

To make chevrons using double crochet, start with a foundation chain that has a multiple of 10 chains, plus 1.

Row 1:

1

In the third chain from your hook, work 1 double crochet. (The skipped chains count as 1 double crochet.)

2

Work 1 double crochet into each of the next 3 chains.

3

Over the next 3 chain stitches, work 3 double crochet stitches together (dc3tog) to decrease.

4

Work 1 double crochet into each of the next 3 chains.

Work 3 double crochets into the next chain.

Repeat steps 2–5 until you reach the last chain.

Work 2 double crochet stitches into the last chain of the row.

Chain 3 for the turning chain (counts as 1 double crochet in the next row) and turn your work so that the opposite side faces you.

Row 2:

1. Work 1 double crochet into the first stitch of the row.
2. Work 1 double crochet into each of the next 3 double crochet stitches.
3. Over the next 3 stitches, work 3 double crochet stitches together (dc3tog) to decrease.
4. Work 1 double crochet into each of the next 3 double crochet stitches.
5. Work 3 double crochet stitches into the next stitch.
6. Repeat steps 2–5 across the second row, ending with 2 double crochet stitches worked into the top of the turning chain. Chain 3 for the turning chain and turn your work.

Repeat row 2 to continue the pattern.

Tip: Depending on how many chain stitches you've done, subsequent rows will sometimes start at a peak and other times at a valley. Just make sure your increases (peaks) and decreases (valleys) in each row line up.

Shell Stitch

Shells are created by working several stitches into the same stitch or space. They are also called fan stitches.

To make shell stitches using single and double crochet, start with a foundation chain that has a multiple of 4 chains, plus 1.

Row 1:

In the fifth chain from your hook, work 4 double crochet stitches.

Skip the next 3 chains and work 4 double crochet stitches into the next chain.

Repeat step 2 across the row until there are 4 chains left. Skip 3 chains and work 2 double crochet stitches into the last chain. Chain 1 for the turning chain and turn your work so that the opposite side faces you.

Row 2:

Work 1 single crochet into each of the double crochet stitches from the previous row. At the end of row 2, chain 3 for the turning chain and turn your work so that the opposite side faces you.

Row 3:

1. Work 1 double crochet into the first stitch. Skip 3 stitches.
2. Work 4 double crochets into the next single crochet stitch. Skip the next 3 single crochet stitches.
3. Repeat step 2 across the row until there are 2 stitches left.
4. Skip the next single crochet stitch and work 1 double crochet into the last stitch.
5. Chain 1 for the turning chain and turn your work so that the opposite side faces you.

Row 4:

1. Work 1 single crochet into the next double crochet.
2. Continue working 1 single crochet into each double crochet stitch across the row.
3. Work 1 single crochet stitch into the top of the turning chain from the previous row.
4. Chain 3 for the turning chain and turn your work so that the opposite side faces you.

Row 5:

1. Skip the first 2 single crochet stitches.
2. Work 4 double crochet stitches into the next single crochet.
3. Skip the next 3 single crochets.
4. Repeat steps 2–3 across the row until there are 2 stitches left.
5. Skip the next stitch and work 1 double crochet stitch into the last stitch of the previous row.
6. Chain 1 for the turning chain and turn your work so that the opposite side faces you.

Repeat rows 4–5 to continue the pattern.

Bobbles

Bobbles work multiple stitches together into 1 stitch or space.

This bobble uses single and double crochet. Start with a foundation chain that has any odd number of chains.

Row 1:

1

In the second chain from your hook, work 1 single crochet stitch.

2

Chain 1. Skip 1 chain and work 1 single crochet stitch into the next chain. Repeat step 2 across the row.

3

At the end of the row, chain 3 for the turning chain and turn your work so the opposite side faces you.

Row 2:

1

Skip the first stitch. (The turning chain counts as the first double crochet in this row.)

Row 2 (continued):

In the next chain space, double crochet 5 together (dc5tog) following the tip instructions.

Tip: **How to double crochet 5 together:**

1. Yarn over. Insert your hook into the chain space.
2. Yarn over and draw the yarn through the space.
3. Yarn over and draw the yarn through the first 2 loops on your hook.
4. Repeat steps 1–3, inserting your hook into the same chain space, until you have 6 loops on your hook. Each time you repeat this process, you will add another loop to your hook.

When you have 6 loops on your hook, yarn over and draw the yarn through all 6 loops on your hook. You will have 1 loop on your hook when your 5 double crochets are complete.

Make 1 chain stitch to secure and complete the bobble.

Repeat steps 2–4 across the row, ending with 1 double crochet in the last single crochet of the row. Chain 1 for the turning chain and turn your work.

Row 3:

1. Work 1 single crochet into the first stitch.
2. Chain 1. Skip 1 chain and work 1 single crochet into the next stitch.
3. Repeat step 2 across the row.

Repeat rows 2–3 to continue the pattern.

Clusters (CL)

You make clusters by combining stitches together into the same stitch or space.

To make cluster stitches using single crochet, start with a foundation chain that has a multiple of 2 chains, plus 1.

Tip: **How to single crochet 2 together using 2 chain spaces:**

1. Insert your hook into the chain space to be worked.
2. Yarn over and draw the yarn through the space. You will have 2 loops on your hook.
3. Insert your hook into the next chain space.
4. Yarn over and draw the yarn through the space. There will be 3 loops on your hook.
5. Yarn over and draw the yarn through all 3 loops on your hook. There will be 1 loop left on your hook.

Row 1:

1 In the second chain from your hook, work 1 single crochet stitch.

2 Chain 1. Skip 1 chain and work 1 single crochet into the next chain. Repeat step 2 across the row. Chain 1 for the turning chain.

Row 2:

Turn your work so that the opposite side faces you. Work 1 single crochet into the first stitch of the row. Chain 1.

Following the tip instructions, single crochet 2 together (sc2tog), working into the next 2 chain spaces. Chain 1 when you're finished.

Insert your hook back into the chain space you just worked in. Single crochet 2 together using this chain space and the next. Chain 1.

Repeat step 3 across the row, ending the row with 1 single crochet in the last stitch. Chain 1 for the turning chain and turn your work so that the opposite side faces you.

Row 3:

1. Work 1 single crochet into the first stitch.
2. Chain 1.
3. Skip 1 chain and work 1 single crochet into the next stitch.
4. Repeat steps 2–3 across the row.

Repeat rows 2–3 to continue the pattern.

Puffs

Puff stitches are similar to bobbles.

To make puffs using half double crochet, start with a foundation chain that has any odd number of chains.

Tip: **How to half double crochet 4 together (hdc4tog):**

1. Yarn over and insert your hook into the chain space.
2. Yarn over and draw the loop through. You will have 3 loops on your hook. It's important to keep your loops taller so it's easier to draw through them at the end.
3. Repeat steps 1–2 two more times until you have 7 loops on your hook. (With every repeat, you add 2 more loops to your hook.)
4. Yarn over and draw through all 7 loops. There will be 1 loop left on your hook.

Row 1:

1

In the second chain from your hook, work 1 single crochet stitch.

2

Chain 1. Skip 1 chain and work 1 single crochet into the next chain. Repeat step 2 across the row.

3 At the end of the row, chain 2 for the turning chain and turn your work so that the opposite side faces you.

Row 2:

1 Skip the first stitch. The turning chain counts as the first half double crochet in this row.

In the next chain space, work 4 half double crochet stitches together (hdc4tog) following the tip instructions, until you have 7 loops on your hook.

Yarn over and draw through all 7 loops on your hook. There will be 1 loop left when your 4 half double crochets are complete.

Chain 1 to secure and complete the puff.

Repeat steps 2–4 across the row, ending with 1 half double crochet in the last stitch of the previous row.

Chain 1 for the turning chain and turn your work so the opposite side faces you.

Row 3:

1. Work 1 single crochet into the first stitch.
2. Chain 1. Skip 1 chain and work 1 single crochet into the next stitch.
3. Repeat step 2 across the row.

Repeat rows 2–3 to continue the pattern.

Basketweave

This basketweave uses alternating front post double crochet (FPdc) and back post double crochet (BPdc) stitches. Post stitches are sometimes called raised stitches.

Start with a foundation chain that has a multiple of 6 chains, plus 4.

Front & Back Posts:

Instead of inserting your hook into a stitch or space, you insert it around the front or back of a post. The stitches are worked the same as usual. The only difference is where your hook is inserted.

Front Posts:

Insert your hook under the post from the front side.

Back Posts:

Insert your hook under the post from the back side.

Row 1:

In the 4th chain from your hook, work 1 double crochet. Continue across the row, working 1 double crochet into each chain.

Chain 2 for the turning chain and turn your work so that the opposite side faces you.

Row 2:

Work 1 double crochet around the 2nd front post of the previous row (FPdc). To do this, yarn over (because you are doing a double crochet) and insert your hook, from the front, under the 2nd post. Finish your double crochet as usual.

Work a FPdc stitch around the next 2 posts so there are a total of 3.

Work 1 double crochet around the next back post (BPdc). To do this, yarn over (because you are doing a double crochet) and insert your hook, from the back side, under the next post. Finish your double crochet as usual.

Work a BPdc stitch around the next 2 posts so there are a total of 3.

Continue across the row, alternating 3 FPdc stitches with 3 BPdc stitches. Finish the row by working 1 double crochet into the top chain of the turning chain.

Chain 2 for the turning chain and turn your work so that the opposite side faces you.

Row 3:

Repeat row 2, alternating 3 FPdc stitches with 3 BPdc stitches across the row. Work 1 double crochet into the top of the turning chain. Chain 2 and turn.

Row 4:

Work 1 BPdc stitch around the 2nd post. Work 1 BPdc stitch around the next 2 posts for a total of 3 BPdc stitches.

Work 1 FPdc stitch around the next 3 posts for a total of 3 FPdc stitches. Continue across the row, alternating 3 BPdc stitches with 3 FPdc stitches.

3. Work 1 double crochet into the top of the last turning chain.

4. Chain 2 for the turning chain and turn your work so that the opposite side faces you.

Row 5:

1. Repeat row 4, alternating 3 BPdc stitches with 3 FPdc stitches across the row. Work 1 double crochet into the top of the turning chain. Chain 2 and turn.

Repeat rows 2–5 to continue the pattern.

Edging Techniques

There are many different edging techniques, which can be crocheted or sewn. Each technique will give your piece a finished and unique look. Here are a few examples.

Shell Stitch Edge

The shells in this example are made from 5 double crochet stitches into the same single crochet stitch. Start with a row of single crochet around the edge of your piece.

Insert your hook into the single crochet stitch in the upper right-hand corner and secure the yarn with a slip stitch. Chain 3.

In the next stitch, work 2 double crochets.

Chain 1. Skip 1 stitch and work 1 single crochet into the next stitch.

Chain 1. Skip 1 stitch and work 5 double crochets into the next stitch. Your first 5-dc shell is complete.

5 Repeat steps 2–4 around your entire piece. End with 3 more double crochets in the same stitch into which you worked the 2 double crochets in step 2 to complete the 5-dc shell.

Picot Stitch Edge

Picot edges can either be made small or large. They can be worked into stitches or spaces and can be added to any row of stitches. Here picots are added to rows of single crochet.

Small Picot

Insert your hook anywhere along the edge and join your edging yarn with a slip stitch.

Chain 3. Insert your hook into the third chain from your hook. Yarn over and draw the yarn through both loops to complete 1 small picot.

Work 1 single crochet into each of the next 3 stitches.

4. Alternate 1 small picot with 3 single crochet stitches around the edges.

Large Picot

1. Insert your hook anywhere along the edge and join your edging yarn with a slip stitch.
2. Chain 5. Insert your hook into the fifth chain from your hook. Yarn over and draw the yarn through both loops to complete 1 large picot.
3. Work 1 single crochet into each of the next 3 stitches.
4. Alternate 1 large picot with 3 single crochet stitches around the edges.

Crab Stitch Edge

Crab stitch is also called reverse single crochet. Start with a row of single crochet along the edge.

Secure the new yarn with a slip stitch in the top left-hand corner.

Insert your hook into the same stitch into which you just worked.

Yarn over and draw the yarn through the stitch (the first loop on your hook). There are 2 loops on your hook.

Yarn over again and draw the yarn through both loops on your hook. You will have 1 loop on your hook when your first crab stitch is complete.

5 Repeat steps 2–4 across the edge, working 1 crab stitch into each single crochet to the right.

Tip: To continue the edging around a corner, work multiple crab stitches into the same corner stitch.

Blanket Stitch Edge

The blanket stitch is sewn rather than crocheted. It lies flat and can help disguise uneven edges.

1. Thread the yarn through the large eye of a tapestry needle. With the wrong side facing up, secure the yarn to the bottom right-hand side of the crochet piece.

2. Flip the crochet piece so the right side is facing up. Draw the needle from back to front through the bottom left-hand side.

3. Insert the needle from front to back through the next small space on the edge.

4. Pull the needle through, going over the loop that was created. You have completed 1 blanket stitch.

5. Continue across the edge, working blanket stitches into the spaces between stitches.

> **Tip:** To continue the edging around a corner, work multiple blanket stitches into the same corner space.

Joining Pieces Together

There are many techniques for joining pieces together, including both crochet and sewing methods. Some methods create a bulkier seam and will be sturdier. Other methods are less bulky, but might be more delicate. Use the same yarn from your project to help disguise the seams. Using a different color yarn makes seams more obvious, but can add more detail to your project.

Single Crochet Join

To join crochet pieces together with single crochet, start by placing the pieces with right sides together and stitches or rows lined up.

Tip: The only difference between a regular row of single crochet stitches and a single crochet join is that you will be working each stitch in both pieces.

Front side

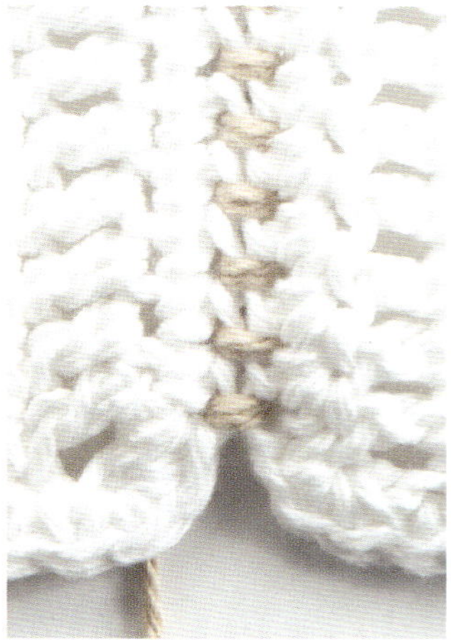

Back side

Insert your hook from front to back under the first pair of stitches on both pieces on the right. Make a slip knot and attach it to the end of your hook.

Draw the slip knot through both pieces, letting the knot catch on the back. Yarn over and draw through the loop on your hook. Yarn over again and draw through both loops on your hook.

3. Insert your hook from front to back under the next pair of stitches on the left and work a single crochet stitch.

4. Repeat step 3 across the seam, working 1 single crochet in each pair of stitches. When complete, fasten off and weave in yarn tails.

Slip Stitch Join

To join crochet pieces with slip stitch, start by placing the pieces with right sides together and stitches or rows lined up.

> **Tip:** To make the slip stitch seam less bulky, try only working through 1 loop of each stitch.

Front side

Back side

Insert your hook from front to back under the first pair of stitches of both pieces on the right. Make a slip knot and attach it to the end of your hook.

Draw the slip knot through both pieces. The knot will catch on the back. Yarn over and draw the yarn through the loop on your hook.

Insert your hook from front to back under the next pair of corresponding stitches on the left. Yarn over and draw the yarn through both loops on your hook. You will have 1 loop on your hook when your first slip stitch is complete.

Repeat step 3 across the seam. When complete, fasten off and weave in yarn tails.

Backstitch Join

The backstitch is a sewing method you can use to join crochet pieces together. It is extra strong, but bulky.

To join 2 crochet pieces with backstitch, start by placing the pieces with right sides together and stitches or rows lined up. Cut a piece of matching yarn to sew with. A piece too long will be difficult to work with.

1 Using a threaded tapestry needle, secure the yarn close to the top right edge. Insert the needle from front to back through both pieces in the first stitch.

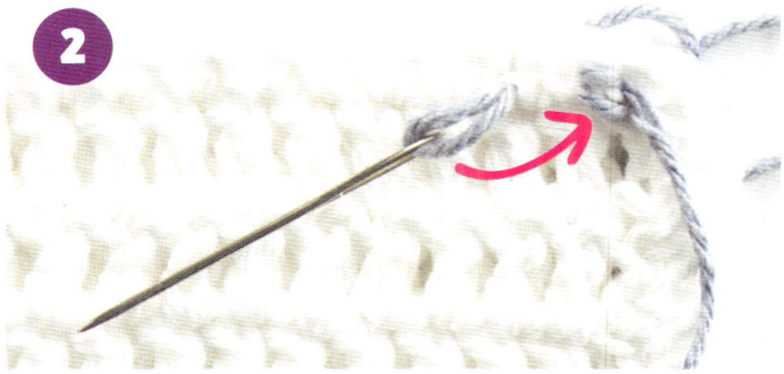

2 From back to front, bring the needle through the next stitch on the left. Draw the yarn through. From front to back, insert the needle into the first stitch and draw through.

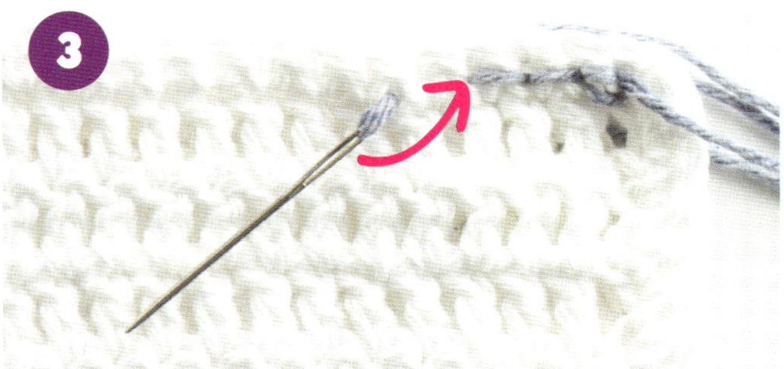

3 Skip the first stitch on the left. From back to front, bring the needle through the next stitch. Draw the yarn through. From front to back, insert the needle into the previous stitch and draw through.

4 Repeat step 3 across the seam. When complete, fasten off and weave in the yarn tails.

Tip: Match the size of your backstitches to the size of the crochet stitches in your project.

Gauge

Gauge refers to how many stitches and rows you should have in a given area in order to match the measurements of a project. The pattern will state how many stitches and rows are needed to achieve the proper gauge. For the projects in this book, gauge is not important. It's most important when making clothing items, like sweaters or socks, in order to get the proper fit.

Four things determine your gauge

- Tension (how loosely or tightly you form the stitches)
- Type and weight of the yarn
- Size of the hook
- Stitch being worked

Making your gauge swatch

Using the same yarn, hook size, and stitch you plan to use for the pattern, crochet a swatch at least 4 x 4 inches. If the project has specific gauge instructions, follow those. After your gauge swatch is complete, lay it on a flat surface.

Measuring your gauge swatch

Use a ruler, measuring tape, or gauge tool and measure 4 inches across your swatch and mark it with pins. Count the number of stitches between the pins. This is your stitch gauge.

Next you will need to measure the row gauge. Place your measuring tool vertically on the swatch, measure 4 inches, and mark it with pins. Count the number of rows between the pins. This is your row gauge.

Adjusting your gauge

If your gauge swatch has too many stitches or rows compared to the pattern, use a larger hook. If your gauge swatch doesn't have enough stitches or rows, use a smaller hook. Keep adjusting your hook size until you have the required gauge.

Tip: The stitch gauge is more important than the row gauge. That's because it is easier to adjust the number of rows than to adjust the number of stitches in your crochet project.

Abbreviations and Symbols

Crochet patterns often use abbreviations and symbols as shorthand to represent frequently used stitches and techniques. Use the guide below as you start to follow patterns using shorthand.

Abbreviations

alt	alternate
approx	approximately
beg	begin/beginning
bet	between
BL or blo	back loop or back loop only
bo	bobble
BP	back post
BPdc	back post double crochet
BPhdc	back post half double crochet
BPsc	back post single crochet
BPtr	back post treble crochet
CC	contrasting color
ch	chain(s)
ch-sp	chain space(s)
CL	cluster
cm	centimeter(s)
cont	continue
dc	double crochet(s)
dec	decrease(s)/decreasing
dtr	double treble crochet(s)
FL or flo	front loop or front loop only
FP	front post
FPdc	front post double crochet
FPhdc	front post half double crochet
FPsc	front post single crochet
FPtr	front post treble crochet
hdc	half double crochet(s)
hk	hook
inc	increase(s)/increasing
lp(s)	loop(s)
MC	main color
mm	millimeter(s)

p	picot
pc	popcorn
pat(s)	pattern(s)
pm	place marker
prev	previous
rem	remain/remaining
rep	repeat(s)
rnd(s)	round(s)
RS	right side
sc	single crochet(s)
sl st	slip stitch
sk	skip
sp(s)	space(s)
st(s)	stitch(es)
tch	turning chain(s)
tog	together
tr	treble crochet(s)
WS	wrong side
yd(s)	yard(s)
yo	yarn over
" or in	inch(es)
[ ]	work instructions within brackets as many times as directed
( )	work instructions within parentheses as many times as directed
*****	repeat the instructions following the single asterisk as directed
******	repeat the instructions between asterisks as many times as directed or repeat from a given set of instructions

Symbols

	chain
	slip stitch
X or +	single crochet
	half double crochet
	double crochet
	treble crochet
	sc2tog
	sc3tog
	dc2tog
	dc3tog
	3-dc cluster
	3-hdc cluster/ puff st/bobble
	5-dc popcorn
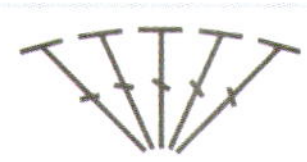	5-dc shell
	ch-3 picot
	front post dc
	back post dc
	worked in back loop only**
	worked in front loop only**

**Symbol appears at base of stitch being worked

Infinity Scarf

Skill Level
BEGINNER

Materials

BULKY 5 1 skein (312 yards)

Hook: 6 mm/U.S. J-10
Other: Tapestry needle

Stitches Used

Chain stitch (ch)
Double crochet (dc)
Slip stitch (sl st)
V-stitch

Instructions

Ch 25.

Row 1: Dc in 4th ch from hook, dc in same st, *skip 2 sts, v-stitch in next st; repeat from * across row. Ch 1, turn.

Row 2: V-stitch in the ch-1 sp from the v-stitch in previous row, *skip 2 spaces, v-stitch in next ch-1 sp; repeat from * across row. Ch 1, turn.

Tip: **How to make the v-stitch:** [dc, ch 1, dc] in one stitch or space.

Rows 3–80 (or desired length): Repeat row 2.

Finishing

Once reaching desired length, fold scarf in half with the 2 short ends together. Join the short ends with a slip stitch through both layers. Fasten off and weave in yarn tails.

Tip: The finished scarf is about 22.5" long and 7" wide when joined.

Starburst Granny Square

Skill Level

EASY

Materials

MEDIUM 4 about 35 yards

Hook: 4.5 mm/U.S. 7
Other: Tapestry needle

Stitches Used

Chain stitch (ch)
Double crochet (dc)
Magic circle
Slip stitch (sl st)

Instructions

Make a magic circle.

Round 1: Ch 3, into magic circle work: 2 dc, ch 3, 3 dc, ch 3, 3 dc, ch 3, 3 dc, ch 3 and join to top of first ch 3 with a sl st.

Round 2: Ch 3, skip the next dc and dc in the last dc of the group from round 1. *In the corner space: 2 dc, ch 3, 2 dc. Dc in the next dc, skip 1 dc and dc in next dc. Repeat from * around and join with sl st to first ch 3 of round.

Round 3: Ch 3, dc in each of the next 3 dc. *In the corner space: 2 dc, ch 3, 2 dc. Dc in each of the next 3 dc, ch 1, dc in each of the next 3 dc. Repeat from * around and join with sl st to first ch 3 of round.

Round 4: Ch 3, dc in each of the next 5 dc. *In the corner space: 2 dc, ch 3, 2 dc. Dc in each of the next 5 dc, ch 1, dc in each of the next 5 dc. Repeat from * around and join with sl st to first ch 3 of round.

Round 5: Ch 3, dc in each of the next 7 dc. *In the corner space: 2 dc, ch 3, 2 dc. Dc in each of the next 7 dc, ch 1, dc in each of the next 7 dc. Repeat from * around and join with sl st to first ch 3 of round. Fasten off and weave in end.

Hat with Pom-Pom

Skill Level
EASY

Materials

BULKY 5 — 1 skein (87 yards)

Hook: 10 mm/U.S. N-15
Other: 2.5" pom-pom maker, scissors, tapestry needle

Stitches Used

Chain stitch (ch)
Half double crochet (hdc)
Half double crochet in back loop only (hdc blo)
Whipstitch

Instructions

Ch 23.

Row 1: Hdc in 2nd ch from hook. Hdc in each ch st across row.

Row 2: Ch 1, turn. Hdc blo in each st across row until last st. Hdc in last st.

Repeat row 2 until rectangle is the correct size to wrap around head with ridges vertical. This hat has 24 rows. Fasten off, leaving a long tail to sew rectangle together.

Finishing

First, fold short sides of rectangle together. Thread the long yarn tail through a tapestry needle. Join short sides of rectangle together using a whipstitch (see pages 78–79).

Next, whipstitch along entire top edge of hat tube. (Do not whipstitch two layers of tube together; only work through one layer.) To do this whipstitch edging, insert threaded tapestry needle from front to back under both loops of stitch at edge. Bring needle up over top and insert from front to back through next stitch on left. Pull tight after every couple stitches to bring top of hat together. Repeat across edge of tube, pulling as tight as possible once reaching point where your whipstitches started to close hole completely. Weave in yarn tails.

Finally, make a pom-pom to top hat.

Tip: Half double crochet in back loop only:
Yarn over and insert hook under back loop only (rather than under both loops) of next stitch, then complete the hdc as usual: yarn over and draw through first loop on hook, yarn over and draw through all 3 loops on hook to complete the hdc blo.

Step 1: Open up both arms of the 2.5" pom-pom maker.

Step 2: Wrap yarn around one arm of pom-pom maker about 35 times. The more wraps, the thicker the pom-pom.

Step 3: Bring yarn across the top of center wheel and begin wrapping around other arm of pom-pom maker.

Step 4: Continue wrapping yarn around second arm until you have the same number of wraps as the first arm (35 times in our example).

Step 5: Close both arms of the pom-pom maker. Cut yarn.

Step 6: Place scissors into the groove on one side and cut through center of one wrapped arm. Repeat for other wrapped arm.

Step 7: Cut a length of yarn about 12" long.

Step 8: Wrap yarn around the pom-pom maker, along the groove where you cut.

Step 9: Tie 2 really tight knots on one side.

Step 10: Wrap yarn around to the other side and tie 2 really tight knots on the other side.

Step 11: Open up arms and pull the halves apart to release pom-pom. You will use 2 long yarn tails to sew pom-pom onto hat.

Step 12: Holding pom-pom by 2 long tails, trim ends to shape into a neat ball.

Tip: The completed hat is about 8.5" across and about 11.5" from the top of the pom-pom to the bottom edge of the hat while lying flat.

Step 13: Thread one of the long yarn tails through a tapestry needle. Insert needle through top of hat on one side of the closed hole.

Step 14: Draw yarn through to inside of hat. Thread other yarn tail through a tapestry needle.

Step 15: Insert needle through top of hat on other side of closed hole. Draw yarn through on inside.

Step 16: On inside of hat, tie yarn tails in 2 knots. Fasten off and trim excess yarn on inside.

Old MacDonald
Peter Rabbit
Three Pigs

Plush Bunny

Skill Level
EASY

Materials

MEDIUM 4 Velvet yarn, 246 yards

Hook: 5 mm/U.S. H-8
Other: Pins, polyfill stuffing, small pom-pom maker, 2 safety eyes (14 mm/0.55"), 1 safety nose (13 mm/0.51"), stitch marker, tapestry needle

Stitches Used

Chain stitch (ch)
Magic circle
Single crochet (sc)
Single crochet 2 together (sc2tog)
Single crochet increase (sc inc)
Slip stitch (sl st)

Instructions

Place the stitch marker in the first stitch of each round. Move the stitch marker up as you work.

Head

Make a magic circle.

Round 1: 6 sc in magic circle.

Round 2: Sc inc in each st around.

Round 3: *Sc, sc inc; repeat from * around.

Round 4: *2 sc, sc inc; repeat from * around.

Round 5: *3 sc, sc inc; repeat from * around.

Round 6: *4 sc, sc inc; repeat from * around.

Round 7: *5 sc, sc inc; repeat from * around.

Round 8: *6 sc, sc inc; repeat from * around.

Round 9: *7 sc, sc inc; repeat from * around.

Rounds 10–20: Sc in each st around.

Adding the Eyes and Nose

1

Step 1: From the front (right) side of the bunny's head, push one of the safety eyes through a space between stitches in rounds 15 and 16 from front to back.

2

Step 2: Attach the plastic washer to the safety eye from the back (wrong) side, inside the bunny's head.

Tip: **How to sc increase:**
Work a single crochet into next stitch. Work another single crochet into that same stitch to complete the sc inc.

Step 3: From the front (right) side of the bunny's head, add other safety eye approximately 8 stitches over from the first eye between rounds 15 and 16 as shown here. From the back (wrong) side, inside the bunny's head, attach washer to 2nd safety eye.

Step 4: From the front (right) side of the bunny's head, insert the safety nose 2 rounds down and centered between the eyes.

Step 5: From the back (wrong) side, inside the bunny's head, attach the plastic washer to the nose.

Tip: Safety eyes and noses:
Safety eyes and noses come in various sizes and colors. They are inserted from the front (right) side like a screw, then a washer is attached on the back (wrong) side to secure them in place. Safety eyes and noses are a nice alternative to buttons, which can be pulled off by young children and present a choking hazard.

After adding safety eyes and nose, begin stuffing head with polyfill as you continue each round.

Round 21: *7 sc, sc2tog; repeat from * around.

Round 22: *6 sc, sc2tog; repeat from * around.

Round 23: *5 sc, sc2tog; repeat from * around.

Round 24: *4 sc, sc2tog; repeat from * around.

Round 25: *3 sc, sc2tog; repeat from * around.

Round 26: *2 sc, sc2tog; repeat from * around.

Round 27: *Sc, sc2tog; repeat from * around.

Round 28: Sc2tog around.

Finish stuffing head with polyfill.

Fasten off, leaving a long tail with which to close the remaining hole and sew the head onto the body later.

Tip: How to sc2tog:
[Insert hook in next stitch, yo, draw yarn through stitch] 2 times, yo, draw yarn through all 3 loops on hook to complete the sc2tog.

Body

The body will begin at the bottom of the legs and work up to the top. Stuff with polyfill as you go.

Make a magic circle.

Round 1: 6 sc in magic circle.

Round 2: Sc inc in each st around.

Round 3: *Sc, sc inc; repeat from * around.

Rounds 4–28: Sc in each st around.

Fasten off. Repeat above for 2nd leg, but do not fasten off after round 28.

Ch 3.

Round 29: Sc into the next stitch of the first leg, and in each stitch around and over the 3 chains to the second leg until you reach your stitch marker.

Rounds 30–45: Sc in each st around.

Round 46: *4 sc, sc2tog; repeat from * around.

Round 47: *3 sc, sc2tog; repeat from * around.

Round 48: *2 sc, sc2tog; repeat from * around.

Round 49: *Sc, sc2tog; repeat from * around.

Round 50: Sc in each st around.

Fasten off.

Arms (make 2)

Stuff arms with polyfill as you go.

Make a magic circle.

Round 1: 6 sc in magic circle.

Rounds 2–22: Sc in each st around.

Fasten off, leaving a long tail with which to sew arms onto body later.

Ears (make 2)

Do not stuff ears.

Make a magic circle.

Round 1: 6 sc in magic circle.

Round 2: Sc inc in each st around.

Round 3: *Sc, sc inc; repeat from * around.

Rounds 4–16: Sc in each st around.

Round 17: Sc2tog in each st around.

Fasten off, leaving a long tail with which to sew ears onto head later.

Tail

Using the 4/medium yarn of your choice and a small pom-pom maker, make a pom-pom tail, following the instructions on pages 61–63 as a guide. We used less than 3 yards of a contrasting white yarn, but you can also use the same velvet yarn as the rest of the bunny. You will have enough leftover velvet yarn from which to make the pom-pom tail. Leave 2 long ends to attach tail to body.

Assembly

Thread the long tail left from the head through a tapestry needle. Sew head securely to body all the way around. Pin arms to body in desired position. Thread long tail from arm through tapestry needle. Sew arms onto body. Pin ears to head in desired position. Thread long tail from ear through tapestry needle. Sew ears onto head. Attach pom-pom tail to back of body using 2 long ends. Weave in all yarn tails when done.

Tip: This completed bunny is about 15" tall from top of head to bottom of legs.

Tip: Stitch markers

Stitch markers are especially critical when crocheting amigurumi. Because you frequently do not join at the end of each round, you need to know exactly which stitch marks the beginning and/or end of each round.

Hobo Purse

Skill Level

EASY

Materials

MEDIUM 4 2 skeins

Hooks: 3.75 mm/U.S. F-5; 4.5 mm/U.S. 7; 5 mm/U.S. H-8; 5.5 mm/U.S. I-9; 6 mm/U.S. J-10

Other: Leather purse strap, tapestry needle

Stitches Used

Chain stitch (ch)

Cluster (CL)

Double crochet (dc)

Single crochet (sc)

Slip stitch (sl st)

Instructions

This pattern, including strap handle loops, is made with 2 strands of yarn together at the same time. (See page 85 for more on multi-strand crochet.)

Start with size 6 mm/U.S. J-10 hook.

Ch 44.

Round 1: 3 dc in 4th ch from hook, *skip 3 sts, 4 dc in next st. Repeat from * to end of row, ch 3 and continue working along opposite side. **4 dc in back loop of previous 4 dc. Repeat from ** to end. Ch 3 and sl st in first dc to join.

Round 2: Sl st to center of first 4-dc cluster. Ch 3, 3 dc in same sp. *4 dc in center of next 4-dc cluster. Repeat from * around, adding 4 dc also in each of the ch 3 turning chains from previous round. Sl st in first dc to join.

Round 3: Sl st to center of first 4-dc cluster. Ch 3, 3 dc in same sp. *4 dc in center of next 4-dc cluster. Repeat from * around. Sl st in first dc to join.

Switch to size 5.5 mm/U.S. I-9 hook.

Rounds 4–6: Repeat round 3.

Switch to size 5 mm/U.S. H-8 hook.

Rounds 7–9: Repeat round 3.

Switch to size 4.5 mm/U.S. 7 hook.

Rounds 10–11: Repeat round 3.

Round 12: Sl st to center of first 4-dc cluster. Ch 3, 2 dc in same sp. *3 dc in center of next 4-dc cluster. Repeat from * around. Sl st in first dc to join.

Switch to size 3.75 mm/U.S. F-5 hook.

Round 13: Sl st to center of first 3-dc cluster. Ch 3, 2 sc in center dc. *3 dc in center dc of next 3-dc cluster. Repeat from * around. Sl st in first dc to join.

Rounds 14–20: Sc in the back loop only of each st around. Fasten off and weave in ends at the end of round 20.

Strap Handle Loops (make 2)

Ch 4.

Row 1: Sc in 2nd ch from hook and in each ch to end of row. Ch 1, turn.

Row 2: Sc in each st across to end of row. Ch 1, turn.

Rows 3–10: Repeat row 2. Fasten off and weave in ends at the end of row 10.

Finishing

With yarn and a tapestry needle, sew the strap handle loops to each side of the bag, centered and even with each other.

Attach the purse strap.

How you attach the purse strap will depend on the type of purse strap. If the purse strap has clips at each end, you can clip the purse handle ends onto the strap handle loops once they are already sewn on securely, with loops already closed. If the purse strap does not have clips, sew one side of the strap handle loop on, put the purse strap in, and then sew the strap handle loop closed. The purse strap used here does not have clips.

Tip: 4-dc clusters

In round 2, the 4-dc clusters referenced are made with the "4 dc in next st" you did in round 1. In round 3, the 4-dc clusters referenced are created any time there are 4 dc stitches made together in round 2.

Tip: 3-dc clusters

In round 13, the 3-dc clusters referenced are made with the "*3 dc in center of next 4-dc cluster" you did in round 12.

Chevron Baby Blanket

Skill Level

EASY

Materials

BULKY 5 — 8 skeins in 2 colors (480 yards of each color)

Hook: 6.5 mm/U.S. K-10.5

Other: Tapestry needle

Stitches Used

Chain stitch (ch)
Double crochet (dc)
Double crochet 3 together (dc3tog)
Slip stitch (sl st)

Instructions

Ch 25.

Row 1: Dc in 4th st from hook, *dc in next 5 sts, dc3tog, dc in next 5 sts, (dc, ch 1, dc) in next st; repeat from * 10 times, ending with 2 dc in the final st.

Row 2: Ch 3, turn. Dc in first st. *Dc in next 5 sts, dc3tog, dc in next 5 sts, (dc, ch 1, dc) in next st; repeat from * 10 times, ending with 2 dc in the final st.

Row 3: Ch 3, turn. Dc in first st. *Dc in next 5 sts, dc3tog, dc in next 5 sts, (dc, ch 1, dc) in next st; repeat from * 10 times, ending with 2 dc in the final st.

Row 4: Change color. Ch 3, turn. Dc in first st. *Dc in next 5 sts, dc3tog, dc in next 5 sts, (dc, ch 1, dc) in next st; repeat from * 10 times, ending with 2 dc in the final st.

Row 5: Ch 3, turn. Dc in first st. *Dc in next 5 sts, dc3tog, dc in next 5 sts, (dc, ch 1, dc) in next st; repeat from * 10 times, ending with 2 dc in the final st.

Row 6: Ch 3, turn. Dc in first st. *Dc in next 5 sts, dc3tog, dc in next 5 sts, (dc, ch 1, dc) in next st; repeat from * 10 times, ending with 2 dc in the final st.

Row 7: Change color. Ch 3, turn. Dc in first st. *Dc in next 5 sts, dc3tog, dc in next 5 sts, (dc, ch 1, dc) in next st; repeat from * 10 times, ending with 2 dc in the final st.

Rows 8 and on: Rep rows 2–7 until desired size. Make sure to end final 3 rows with the same color you started with. Fasten off.

Edging

Join your starting color to first raw edge of blanket and work a single row of dc evenly. Sl st to close and fasten off. Join your starting color to 2nd raw edge of blanket and work a single row of dc evenly. Sl st to close and fasten off. Weave in ends.

Tip: Double crochet 3 together (dc3tog)

1. Yarn over. Insert your hook into the stitch.
2. Yarn over and draw the yarn through the stitch.
3. Yarn over and draw the yarn through the first 2 loops on your hook.
4. Repeat steps 1–3 two times, inserting your hook into the same stitch. You will have 4 loops on your hook.
5. Yarn over and draw through all 4 loops on your hook. There will be 1 loop left when dc3tog is complete.

Frog

Skill Level

EASY

Materials

MEDIUM 4 — 364-yard skein in green (you'll have yarn leftover), plus 6–8" of black scrap yarn for mouth

Hook: 4 mm/U.S. G-6

Other: Pins, polyfill stuffing, 13 mm safety eyes, stitch marker, tapestry needle

Stitches Used

Chain stitch (ch)
Magic circle
Single crochet (sc)
Single crochet 2 together (sc2tog)
Slip stitch (sl st)

Instructions

Use a stitch marker to mark the beginning of each round.

Eyes (make 2)

Make a magic circle.

Round 1: 8 sc in magic circle.

Round 2: *2 sc in next st, sc in each of next 3 sts; repeat from * around.

Round 3: 2 sc in next st, sc in next 2 sts, 2 sc in next st, sc in next 6 sts.

Fasten off after first eye. Do not fasten off after second eye.

Connecting the Eyes

Step 1: While still attached to 2nd eye, ch 4.

Step 2: Slip stitch in last stitch of first eye.

Step 3: Single crochet in each stitch around first eye until you reach ch 4.

Step 4: Single crochet in the back bumps only of 4 ch stitches.

Step 5: Sc in first st of 2nd eye and in each st around until you reach middle ch 4 sts.

Step 6: Sc in each of middle ch 4 sts.

Step 7: Continue to sc in each st around.

Head/Body

The head/body builds off the connected eyes.

Round 1: Sc in each st around, making the sc sts in the top of middle ch 4 sts.

Round 2: 2 sc in each of next 3 sts, sc in next 17 sts, 2 sc in each of next 3 sts, sc in next 9 sts.

Round 3: 2 sc in next st, sc in each of next 7 sts, 2 sc in next st, sc in each of next 8 sts, 2 sc in next st, sc in each of next 8 sts, 2 sc in next st, sc in each of next 11 sts.

Rounds 4–10: Sc in each st around. Add two 13 mm safety eyes. (See pages 65–66 for more on adding safety eyes.) Begin stuffing with polyfill as you go.

Round 11: *Sc2tog, sc in each of next 5 sts; repeat from * around.

Round 12: *2 sc in next st, sc in each of next 5 sts; rep from * around.

Round 13: *2 sc in next st, sc in each of next 6 sts; rep from * around.

Round 14: *2 sc in next st, sc in each of next 7 sts; rep from * around.

Rounds 15–22: Sc in each st around.

Round 23: *Sc2tog, sc in each of next 7 sts; repeat from * around.

Round 24: *Sc2tog, sc in each of next 6 sts; repeat from * around.

Round 25: *Sc2tog, sc in each of next 5 sts; repeat from * around.

Round 26: *Sc2tog, sc in each of next 4 sts; repeat from * around.

Round 27: *Sc2tog, sc in each of next 3 sts; repeat from * around.

Round 28: *Sc2tog, sc in each of next 2 sts; repeat from * around. Finish firmly stuffing.

Round 29: *Sc2tog, sc in next st; rep from * around.

Round 30: Sc2tog in each st around.

Fasten off and stitch bottom closed. Weave in ends.

Legs (make 2)

Do not stuff legs. Make a magic circle.

Round 1: 6 sc in magic circle.

Round 2: 2 sc in each st around.

Rounds 3–5: Sc in each st around.

Round 6: *Sc2tog, sc in next st; rep from * around.

Rounds 7–22: Sc in each st around.
Fasten off, leaving long tail for sewing.

Arms (make 2)

Do not stuff arms. Make a magic circle.

Round 1: 6 sc in magic circle.

Round 2: *2 sc in next st, sc in each of next 2 sts; rep from * around.

Rounds 3–14: Sc in each st around.
Fasten off, leaving long tail for sewing.

Assembly

Pin both arms and legs in desired position. With a tapestry needle threaded with yarn tail, sew each arm and leg onto frog body. With strand of black scrap yarn, sew mouth on frog.

Headband

Skill Level

BEGINNER

Materials

MEDIUM 4 less than 1 skein (210 yards)

Hook: 5 mm/U.S. H-8
Other: Tapestry needle

Stitches Used

Chain stitch (ch)
Double crochet (dc)
Single crochet (sc)
Slip stitch (sl st)

Instructions

Ch 44.

Row 1: 2 dc in 3rd ch from hook, *sk 2 ch, sc in next ch, ch 2, 2 dc in same st; rep from * to end of row. Sc in last ch.

Row 2: Ch 2, turn. 2 dc in next st, *sc in ch-2 sp, ch 2, 2 dc in same sp; rep from * to end of row. Sc in top tch of prev row.

Row 3: Rep row 2.

Row 4: Rep row 2. Ch 30, sl st to the other end of the headband, creating a circle. Sl st across the short end of the headband to edge, ch 30, sl st to the other end of headband (where you started) and fasten off.

Tip: Depending on your head size, increase or decrease the number of chain stitches in row 4.

Chunky Mittens

Skill Level
INTERMEDIATE

Materials

SUPER BULKY 6 — 2 skeins (212 yards total)

Hooks: 8 mm/U.S. L-11, 9 mm/U.S. M-13
Other: Tapestry needle

Stitches Used

Chain stitch (ch)
Half double crochet (hdc)
Half double crochet in back loop only (hdc blo)
Herringbone half double crochet (Hhdc)
Herringbone half double crochet increase (Hhdc inc)
Single crochet (sc)
Single crochet 2 together (sc2tog)
Slip stitch (sl st)
Whipstitch

Instructions

Mitten Cuffs (make 2)

With a size 8 mm/U.S. L-11 hook, ch 15.

Row 1: Hdc in 3rd ch from hook. Hdc in each ch st across row. Ch 2, turn.

Rows 2–11: Hdc blo in each st across row. Ch 2, turn.

Row 12: Hdc blo in each st across row. Fasten off, leaving a 12" tail to join cuff with a whipstitch.

Tip: **How to hdc blo:**
Yo, insert hook under back loop only of next stitch, yo, draw through first loop on hook, yo, draw through all 3 loops on hook.

Tip: The finished mittens are about 14" from top of mitten to bottom edge with cuffs unrolled.

Joining with a Whipstitch

Step 1: Thread tapestry needle with 12" yarn tail.

Step 2: Fold short ends of the cuff together so that stitches on both edges are lined up.

Step 3: Insert needle from front to back under the first stitch on each piece.

Step 4: Bring the needle around and insert from front to back under the next pair of stitches.

Step 5: Repeat for each pair of stitches across the seam. Fasten off and weave in yarn tail.

Right and Left Mittens

Using a size 9 mm/U.S. M-13 hook, attach yarn anywhere along one edge of the cuff. Instead of working around in the same direction, you will turn after each round.

Round 1: Ch 2, 12 Hhdc evenly around the cuff, sl st in first Hhdc to join. Ch 2, turn.

Round 2: 5 Hhdc, Hhdc inc, Hhdc inc, 5 Hhdc, sl st in first Hhdc to join. Ch 2, turn.

Round 3: 6 Hhdc, Hhdc inc, Hhdc inc, 6 Hhdc, sl st in first Hhdc to join. Ch 2, turn.

Round 4: 7 Hhdc, Hhdc inc, Hhdc inc, 7 Hhdc, sl st in first Hhdc to join. Ch 2, turn.

For rounds 5–14, work one mitten following instructions for right mitten and the other mitten following instructions for left mitten.

Right Mitten

Round 5: 7 Hhdc, ch 2, skip next 5 Hhdc, Hhdc in each of the remaining 6 Hhdc, sl st in first Hhdc to join. Ch 2, turn.

Round 6: Hhdc in each st around (including ch 2 from previous round), sl st in first Hhdc to join. Ch 2, turn.

Rounds 7–12: Hhdc in each st around, sl st in first Hhdc to join. Ch 2, turn.

Round 13: 6 Hhdc, Hhdc2tog, 5 Hhdc, Hhdc2tog, sl st in first Hhdc to join. Ch 2, turn.

Round 14: 5 Hhdc, Hhdc2tog, 4 Hhdc, Hhdc2tog, sl st in first Hhdc to join. Fasten off, leaving a 12" tail to close top of mitten.

Left Mitten

Round 5: 6 Hhdc, ch 2, skip next 5 Hhdc, Hhdc in each of the remaining 7 Hhdc, sl st in first Hhdc to join. Ch 2, turn.

Round 6: Hhdc in each st around (including ch 2 from previous round), sl st in first Hhdc to join. Ch 2, turn.

Rounds 7–12: Hhdc in each st around, sl st in first Hhdc to join. Ch 2, turn.

Round 13: 5 Hhdc, Hhdc2tog, 6 Hhdc, Hhdc2tog, sl st in first Hhdc to join. Ch 2, turn.

Round 14: 4 Hhdc, Hhdc2tog, 5 Hhdc, Hhdc2tog, sl st in first Hhdc to join. Fasten off, leaving a 12" tail to close top of mitten.

Tip: **How to sc2tog:**
Insert hook in next stitch, yo, draw yarn through stitch, insert hook in next stitch, yo, draw yarn through stitch, yo, draw through all 3 loops on hook to complete.

Tip: **How to Hhdc:**
Yo and insert hook into indicated stitch. Yo and pull up a loop by drawing yarn through stitch. You now have 3 loops on hook. Draw that first loop on hook through 2nd loop on hook. You now have 2 loops on hook. Yo and draw through remaining 2 loops on hook to complete the Hhdc.

Tip: **How to Hhdc increase:**
Work a Hhdc in next stitch of previous round, inserting hook under top 2 loops of stitch. Work another Hhdc in that same stitch to complete the Hhdc inc.

Tip: **How to Hhdc2tog:**
Yo and insert hook under front loop of next stitch, then insert your hook under front loop of next stitch after that without yarning over again (4 loops on hook), yo and draw through first 3 loops on hook (2 loops left on hook), yo and draw through remaining 2 loops on hook to complete the Hhdc2tog.

Closing the Mitten Tops

Thread 12" yarn tail through a tapestry needle. Working in the front loops only of each Hhdc around and from inside the mitten out, stitch loosely around in each stitch. Gently cinch together to close top of mitten. Weave in remaining tail.

Thumb

Using a size 9 mm/U.S. M-13 hook, attach yarn at the right corner of the thumb where rounds 4 and 5 meet. Work counterclockwise.

Round 1: Ch 1, sc2tog, sc, sc2tog, sl st to corner between rounds 4 and 5, 3 sc, sl st to opposite corner between rounds 4 and 5, sl st in top of first sc to join.

Rounds 2–4: Ch 1, sc in each sc around, sl st in top of first sc to join.

Round 5: Ch 1, sc in each sc around, sl st in top of first sc to join. Fasten off, leaving a 12" tail to close top of thumb.

Close top of thumb the same way you closed top of mittens.

Granny Market Bag

Skill Level: EASY

Materials

MEDIUM 4 in 2 colors (372 yards of each color)

Hook: 4 mm/U.S. G-6

Other: 4 stitch markers, tapestry needle

Stitches Used

Chain stitch (ch)

Double crochet (dc)

Magic circle

Single crochet (sc)

Slip stitch (sl st)

Instructions

Using color 1 (here in tan), make a magic circle.

Round 1: Working into magic circle: ch 3, 3 dc, *(ch 2, 4 dc); rep from * 3 times. Sl st to top of first ch 3 to close round.

Round 2: Ch 3, (dc, ch 2, 2 dc) into ch-2 sp, dc in each st around, working (2 dc, ch 2, 2 dc) in each ch-2 sp. Sl st in top of first ch 3 to close round.

Round 3: Ch 3, dc in each st around, working (2 dc, ch 2, 2 dc) in each ch-2 sp. Sl st in top of first ch 3 to close round.

Rounds 4–11: Repeat round 3. At the end of round 11, fasten off and weave in yarn tails.

Counting in from 2 corner ch-2 spaces, place a stitch marker in the center 2 stitches of that round and repeat for all 4 sides (you will need 4 stitch markers).

Using color 1 (tan) again, attach in any corner ch-2 sp to begin round 12.

Round 12: Ch 3, (dc, ch 2, 2 dc) into ch-2 sp, *dc in each st until 1 st before the marker, skip 4 sts, dc in each st until next ch-2 sp, (2 dc, ch 2, 2 dc) in each ch-2 sp; rep from * around. Sl st in top of first ch 3 to close round.

Round 13: Ch 3, dc in each st around, skipping the 4 middle sts of each side and working (2 dc, ch 2, 2 dc) in each ch-2 sp. Sl st in top of first ch 3 to close round. Fasten off and weave in tails.

Change to color 2 (here in royal blue) and attach in any corner ch-2 sp to begin round 14.

Round 14: Ch 3, (dc, ch 2, 2 dc) into ch-2 sp, dc in each st around, skipping the middle 4 sts of each side and working (2 dc, ch 2, 2 dc) in each ch-2 sp. Sl st in top of first ch 3 to close round.

Rounds 15–21: Ch 3, dc in each st around, skipping the middle 4 sts of each side and working (2 dc, ch 2, 2 dc) in each ch-2 sp. Sl st in top of first ch 3 to close round. Fasten off and weave in tails after the end of round 21.

skipped 4 middle stitches

Change to color 1 (tan) and attach in any corner ch-2 sp to begin round 22.

Round 22: Ch 3, (dc, ch 2, 2 dc) into ch-2 sp, dc in each st around, skipping the middle 4 sts of each side and working (2 dc, ch 2, 2 dc) in each ch-2 sp. Sl st in top of first ch 3 to close round.

Round 23: Ch 3, dc in each st around, skipping the middle 4 sts of each side and working (2 dc, ch 2, 2 dc) in each ch-2 sp. Sl st in top of first ch 3 to close round. Fasten off and weave in tails.

Change to color 2 (royal blue) and attach in any corner ch-2 sp to begin round 24.

Round 24: Ch 3, (dc, ch 2, 2 dc) into ch-2 sp, dc in each st around, skipping the middle 4 sts of each side and working (2 dc, ch 2, 2 dc) in each ch-2 sp. Sl st in top of first ch 3 to close round.

Rounds 25–27: Ch 3, dc in each st around, skipping the middle 4 sts of each side and working (2 dc, ch 2, 2 dc) in each ch-2 sp. Sl st in top of first ch 3 to close round. Fasten off and weave in tails after the end of round 27.

Change to color 1 (tan) and attach in any corner ch-2 sp to begin round 28.

Round 28: Ch 3, (dc, ch 2, 2 dc) into ch-2 sp, dc in each st around, skipping middle 4 sts of each side and working (2 dc, ch 2, 2 dc) in each ch-2 sp. Sl st in top of first ch 3 to close round. Fasten off and weave in tails.

Tip: The finished bag is about 13" wide and just under 18" tall from the base to a top peak. Each strap is about 17" long.

Straps

Using color 1 (tan), attach in any corner ch-2 sp and ch 60. Join with a sl st to the next corner ch-2 sp and fasten off.

Repeat above for 2nd strap, using remaining 2 corner ch-2 sp. Do not fasten off after joining with a sl st to the corner ch-2 sp.

Round 1: Ch 1, sc in each st around and into each ch of the straps. Sl st into the first sc to join and end round. Fasten off and weave in tails.

Potholder

Skill Level
BEGINNER

Materials

MEDIUM 4 less than 1 skein (210 yards)

Hook: 6.5 mm/U.S. K-10.5
Other: Tapestry needle

Stitches Used

Chain stitch (ch)
Half double crochet (hdc)
Slip stitch (sl st)

Instructions

Work pattern using 2 strands of yarn held together at the same time, treating the 2 strands as 1 strand. This will create a thicker potholder. Both strands of yarn are coming from the same skein for this project. Pull 1 strand from the center of the skein and 1 strand from the outside of the skein.

Ch 20.

Row 1: Sl st in 2nd ch from hook. *Hdc, sl st; repeat from * across row. Ch 1, turn.

Rows 2–22: Sl st in first st, *hdc, sl st; repeat from * across row. Ch 1, turn.

Ch 10. Sl st into base of ch 10 to create a loop.

Fasten off and weave in yarn tails.

Tip: The finished potholder is about 8" by 8".

Tip: Because this pattern is worked with 2 strands of yarn held together, each yarn over and resulting loop on your hook will consist of 2 strands. Treat each set of 2 loops on your hook as 1 loop regardless of which stitch you are performing.

Circular Blanket

Skill Level

EASY

Materials

MEDIUM 4 — 4 skeins (1 of each color)

Hook: 5 mm/U.S. H-8
Other: Tapestry needle

Stitches Used

Chain stitch (ch)
Cluster (CL)
Double crochet (dc)
Magic circle
Single crochet (sc)
Slip stitch (sl st)

Instructions

Start with color 1. Change colors every 3 rounds, or as desired.

Make a magic circle.

Round 1: Ch 3, 13 dc into magic circle. Join with a sl st to top of first dc.

Round 2: Ch 2, 2 dc in each dc around. Join with a sl st to top of first dc.

Round 3: Ch 1, sc in same st, ch 3. *Skip next dc, sc in next dc, ch 3. Repeat from * around. Join with a sl st to first sc.

Round 4: Sl st into ch-3 space, (ch 3, 2 dc) in same space, ch 1. (3 dc, ch 1) in each ch-3 space around. Join with a sl st to top of beginning ch 3.

Round 5: Sl st into next dc, (ch 3, 2 dc) in same dc, ch 2. (3 dc, ch 2) in middle dc of each 3-dc cluster around. Join with a sl st to top of beginning ch 3.

Round 6: Sl st into next dc, (ch 3, 2 dc) in same dc, ch 1, dc in ch-2 space, ch 1. *3 dc in center dc of next 3-dc cluster, ch 1, dc in ch-2 space, ch 1. Repeat from * around. Join with a sl st in top of beginning ch 3.

Round 7: Sl st into next dc, (ch 3, 2 dc) in same dc, ch 1, 3 dc in next dc, ch 1. *3 dc in center dc of next 3-dc cluster, ch 1, 3 dc in next dc, ch 1. Repeat from * around. Join with a sl st in top of beginning ch 3.

Round 8: Sl st into next dc, (ch 3, 2 dc) in same dc, ch 1, (3 dc, ch 1) in center dc of each 3-dc cluster around. Join with a sl st in top of beginning ch 3.

Rounds 9–10: Repeat round 5.

Tip: Using a bulkier yarn weight will create a larger blanket.

Tip: The clusters are made from each (3 dc) grouping.

Round 11: Repeat round 6.

Round 12: Sl st into next dc, (ch 3, 2 dc) in same dc, ch 1, dc in next dc, ch 1. *3 dc in center dc of next 3-dc cluster, ch 1, dc in next dc, ch 1. Repeat from * around. Join with a sl st in top of beginning ch 3.

Round 13: Repeat round 7.

Rounds 14–17: Repeat round 8.

Rounds 18–19: Repeat round 5.

Round 20: Repeat round 6.

Rounds 21–24: Repeat round 12.

Round 25: Repeat round 7.

Rounds 26–28: Repeat round 8.

Round 29: Ch 1, sc in same st, sc in each dc and ch-1 space around. Join with a sl st to first sc.

Round 30: Sl st into next sc, (ch 3, 3 dc) in same sc, skip next sc, sc in next sc, skip next sc. *4 dc in next sc, skip next sc, sc in next sc, skip next sc. Repeat from * around. Join with a sl st to top of beginning ch 3. Fasten off and weave in ends.

Ridged Baby Bib

Skill Level

EASY

Materials

MEDIUM 4 Cotton yarn, less than 200 yards

Hook: 5 mm/U.S. H-8
Other: 2 half-inch buttons, pins or stitch markers (optional), tapestry needle

Stitches Used

Chain stitch (ch)
Single crochet (sc)
Single crochet in back loop only (sc blo)
Single crochet 2 together in back loops only (sc2tog blo)
Slip stitch (sl st)

Instructions

Ch 57.

Row 1: Sc in 2nd ch from hook and in each ch st across row.

Row 2: Ch 1, turn. *Sc blo in next 13 sc, 2 sc blo in next sc; rep from * to end of row.

Row 3: Ch 2, turn. *Sc blo in next 14 sc, 2 sc in next sc; rep from * to end of row.

Row 4 (buttonhole row): Ch 1, turn. Sc blo in next 2 sc, ch 1, sk next sc (first buttonhole), sc blo in next 6 sc, ch 1, sk next sc (2nd buttonhole), sc blo in next 5 sc, 2 sc blo in next sc. *Sc blo in next 15 sc, 2 sc blo in next sc; rep from * to end of row.

Row 5: Ch 1, turn. *Sc blo in next 16 sc, 2 sc blo in next sc; rep from * to end of row.

Row 6: Ch 1, turn. *Sc blo in next 17 sc, 2 sc blo in next sc; rep from * to end of row.

Row 7: Ch 1, turn. *Sc blo in next 18 sc, 2 sc blo in next sc; rep from * to end of row.

Row 8: Ch 1, turn. Sl st in next 20 sc, sc blo in next sc, sc2tog blo, sc blo in next 16 sc, [2 sc blo in next sc] twice, sc blo in next 16 sc, sc2tog blo, sc blo in next sc. Remaining sc in row will stay unworked.

Row 9: Ch 1, turn. Sc blo in first sc, sc2tog blo, sc blo in next 16 sc, [2 sc blo in next sc] twice, sc blo in next 16 sc, sc2tog blo, sc blo in last sc.

Rows 10–126: Repeat row 9. Fasten off and weave in yarn tails.

Tip: **How to sc blo:**
Insert hook under back loop only (rather than under both top loops) of next stitch, then complete the sc as usual: yo and draw yarn through first loop on hook, yo and draw yarn through both loops on hook to complete the sc blo.

Tip: **How to sc2tog blo:**
Insert hook under back loop only of next stitch, yo and draw through stitch (2 loops on hook), insert hook under back loop only of next stitch (3 loops on hook), yo and draw through all 3 loops on hook to complete the sc2tog blo.

Sewing on the Buttons

Sew buttons in place on strap opposite buttonhole strap. Position straps so buttonholes overlap strap where you'll sew on buttons. Mark where buttons will go with pins or stitch markers, if desired. Place first button in center of collar strap, and second button about 1¾" up from first button (or whatever the correct distance is for your bib).

Step 1: Thread tapestry needle with matching yarn. If holes in buttons are too narrow for a tapestry needle, use a sewing needle and thread.

Step 2: Insert needle from the back (wrong) side of the bib up through 1 button hole to the front (right) side, leaving a tail on the back side.

Step 3: Insert needle from front to back through the other button hole. Pull tight.

Step 4: Insert needle from back to front through the first button hole again. Insert needle from front to back through other button hole. Repeat until you feel button is secure.

Step 5: On the back (wrong) side, trim yarn. Tie a knot with the yarn tails.

Step 6: Tie a second tight knot to secure. Trim or weave in yarn tails.

Round Handle Purse

Skill Level

INTERMEDIATE

Materials

SUPER BULKY 6 — 3 skeins

Hook: 8 mm/U.S. L-11
Other: 2 round handles, stitch markers, tapestry needle

Stitches Used

Chain stitch (ch)
Front post double crochet (FPdc)
Half double crochet (hdc)
Single crochet (sc)
Slip stitch (sl st)

Instructions

Make 2 pieces. Ch 41.

Row 1: Hdc in 3rd ch from hook and in each st across. Ch 1, turn.

Row 2: Sc in each st across. Ch 2, turn.

Row 3: *Hdc in next 4 sts, FPdc, hdc in next st, FPdc. Repeat from * across, ending with hdc in last 4 sts. Ch 1, turn.

Row 4: Repeat row 2.

Row 5: *Hdc in next 4 sts, skip first FPdc from row 3 and FPdc around 2nd FPdc, ch 1, FPdc over skipped FPdc. Rep from * across, ending with hdc in last 4 sts. Ch 1, turn.

Row 6: Repeat row 2.

Row 7: *Hdc in next 4 sts, FPdc around first FPdc from prev row, hdc in next st, FPdc around next FPdc. Rep from * across, ending with hdc in last 3 sts. Ch 1, turn.

Continue repeating rows 2–7 until desired size. Fasten off and weave in ends.

Finishing

Hold 2 pieces together with wrong sides facing out. Start at one top edge, and sc both sides together, continuing along the bottom edge and up opposite edge. Fasten off and weave in ends.

Turn right side out.

Begin at one side of purse and sc in first 2 sts, then begin working sc around the handle to attach the handle to the purse. Continue working sc sts around handle and across purse until the final 2 sts, sc in each final st. Continue the same way across the opposite side so both handles are attached. Sl st to join with initial sc. Fasten off and weave in ends.

Crochet Shrug

Skill Level
EASY

Materials

BULKY 5 900 yards

Hook: 8 mm/U.S. L-11
Other: Tapestry needle

Stitches Used

Chain stitch (ch)
Half double crochet (hdc)
Single crochet (sc)
Whipstitch

Instructions

Ch 100.

Row 1: Hdc in 3rd ch from hook and in each ch st across row. Ch 1, turn.

Rows 2–4: Hdc in each st across row. Ch 1, turn.

Row 5: *(Sc, ch 1, sc) in next st, sk next st; rep from * across until last st. Sc in last st. Ch 1, turn.

Rows 6–65: *(Sc, ch 1, sc) in next ch-1 sp; rep from * across until last st. Sc in last st. Ch 1, turn.

Row 66: *Hdc in next ch-1 sp, sk next sc, hdc in next sc; rep from * across row. Ch 1, turn.

Rows 67–70: Hdc in each st across row. Ch 1, turn. After final row, fasten off and weave in yarn tails.

whipstitch seam

Finishing

You will now have a rectangle that is roughly 40″ wide and 27″ tall. Lay out rectangle and fold in each corner halfway to meet the other evenly. Leave an opening 9″ across for each arm hole. Using matching yarn and a tapestry needle, whipstitch (see pages 78–79) remaining seam where short ends meet to create arm holes on both sides. Weave in all yarn tails when done.

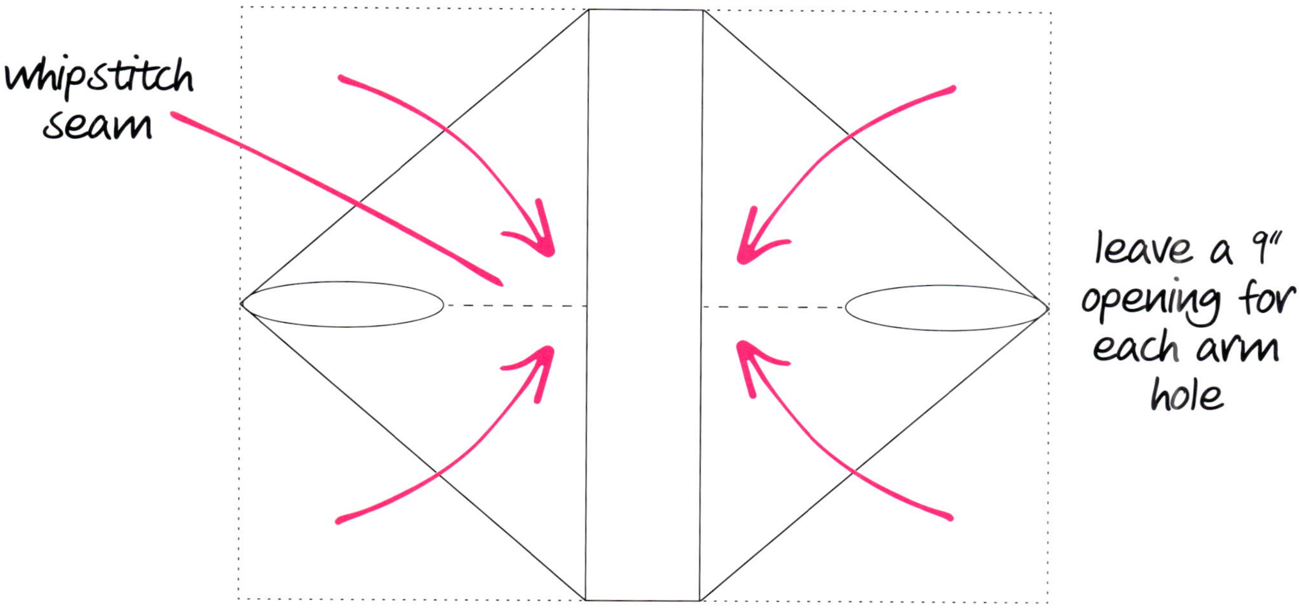

Removable Pillow Cover

Skill Level

EASY

Materials

SUPER BULKY 6 2 skeins (87 yards each)

Hook: 6 mm/U.S. J-10

Other: 12″ x 12″ pillow form, 12″ zipper, pins, sewing needle, tapestry needle, thread

Stitches Used

Chain stitch (ch)
Half double crochet (hdc)
Slip stitch (sl st)
Whipstitch

Instructions

This removable pillow cover is worked in rounds, creating a large tube.

Ch 72. Join with a sl st to the first chain you made to form a ring.

Round 1: Ch 2, sl st in next ch. *Hdc in next ch, sl st in next ch; repeat from * around. Join with a sl st in top of beginning ch 2. Ch 2, turn.

Round 2: Sl st in next hdc. *Hdc in next ch, sl st in next ch; repeat from * around. Join with a sl st in top of beginning ch 2. Ch 2, turn.

Repeat round 2 until size of cover matches size of pillow. This pillow cover is 32 rounds.

Fasten off and weave in yarn tails.

Finishing

Whipstitch one open end of the tube closed using yarn and a tapestry needle. (See pages 78–79.) Sew a zipper into the other open end of the tube.

Tip: **How to whipstitch:**
Hold sides of pillow cover tube with right sides (outward-facing) together and stitches lined up. Insert threaded yarn needle from front to back under the first pair of stitches on the right. Draw yarn through, leaving a tail to weave in later. Bring needle back around and insert from front to back under the next pair of stitches on the left. Repeat for each pair of stitches across the seam. Fasten off and weave in yarn tails.

Sewing in the Zipper

Step 1: Pin one side of the closed zipper, right side facing out, to one inside (wrong side) edge of the pillow cover.

Step 2: Thread a sewing needle with a long piece of matching thread and knot one end. Beginning on the inside (wrong side) at one end, sew zipper onto pillow cover using a running stitch.

Step 3: Continue sewing a running stitch across to end of zipper. Tie a knot and trim excess thread.

Step 4: Pin other side of closed zipper to opposite edge of pillow cover as shown. Open zipper once it's pinned in place and sew onto inside edge of pillow cover with a running stitch as you did for first side.

Step 5: After the zipper is sewn in, add the 12″ x 12″ pillow form to complete the project.

Slouch Hat

Skill Level

EASY

Materials

MEDIUM 4 — 2 skeins

Hook: 4.5 mm/U.S. 7

Other: Tapestry needle

Stitches Used

Chain stitch (ch)
Puff stitch (puff st)
Single crochet (sc)
Single crochet in front loop only (sc flo)
Slip stitch (sl st)

Instructions

Hat band

Ch 11.

Row 1: Sc in 2nd ch from hook and in each ch to end of row.

Row 2: Ch 2, turn. Sc flo across row.

Rows 3 and on: Rep row 2. Cont with the sc flo rows until the band measures about 22″, or to fit comfortably around your head. Fasten off, leaving a tail to sew ends of band together. Use a tapestry needle to sew ends of band together to create a circle.

Hat body

Make a slip knot and push hook through first sc where the band was sewn up. Ch 1, sc all around band. Join with sl st in first ch.

Round 1: Ch 2, *puff st, ch 1, skip 1 st; repeat from * around.

Round 2: Working around continuously, work *puff st in ch-1 sp from prev rnd, ch 1, skip 1 st; repeat from * around.

Rounds 3–20 (or desired size of hat): Rep rnd 2.

Finishing

Seam it up. Don't connect last rnd. Insert hook in front of hat and sc to connect. It will make a figure 8 shape. Turn hat, insert hook in center side of hat, and sc to connect. Turn hat, insert hook in center side of hat, and sc to connect. It will now have a star shape. Cont turning and sc to connect until the top of hat is closed enough to your liking. Fasten off and weave in yarn tails.

Tip: **How to make the puff stitch:**
To make the puff stitch, yarn over and insert your hook in the stitch, yarn over and draw the loop through, [yarn over and insert your hook into the same place] repeat until there are 7 loops on your hook. Yarn over and draw the yarn through all 7 loops.

Cactus

Skill Level

EASY

Materials

MEDIUM 4 120 yards of brown, 120 yards of green, plus scraps of pink for flowers

Hook: 3.5 mm/U.S. E-4

Other: Polyfill stuffing, stitch marker, tapestry needle

Stitches Used

Chain stitch (ch)

Double crochet (dc)

Magic circle

Single crochet (sc)

Single crochet 2 together (sc2tog)

Single crochet in back loop only (sc blo)

Single crochet increase (sc inc)

Slip stitch (sl st)

Treble crochet (tr)

Whipstitch

Instructions

Place a stitch marker in the first stitch of each round and move it up as you work.

Soil

Using brown yarn, make a magic circle.

Round 1: 6 sc in the magic circle.

Round 2: Sc inc in each st around.

Round 3: *Sc, sc inc; repeat from * around.

Round 4: *2 sc, sc inc; repeat from * around.

Round 5: *3 sc, sc inc; repeat from * around.

Round 6: *4 sc, sc inc; repeat from * around.

Rounds 7–15: Sc in each st around.

Round 16: *4 sc, sc2tog; repeat from * around.

Round 17: *3 sc, sc2tog; repeat from * around.

Round 18: *2 sc, sc2tog; repeat from * around.

Tip: The completed cactus fits perfectly in a small flower pot or bowl and never needs watering!

Stuff generously with polyfill.

Round 19: *Sc, sc2tog; repeat from * around.

Round 20: *Sc2tog; repeat from * around.

Fasten off and weave in yarn tails.

Cactus

Using green yarn, ch 16.

Row 1: Sc in 2nd ch from hook, sc in each ch st across row. Ch 1, turn.

Rows 2–24 (or until rectangle is 5.5″ across): Sc blo in each st across row. Ch 1, turn.

Fasten off, leaving a long 20″ tail after last row for the drawstring closure on the top, the whipstitch seam along the side, and the drawstring closure on the bottom of the cactus.

First, thread the 20″ tail through a tapestry needle. Working along the long edge of the rectangle, sew through the top sides (loops) of the stitches along edge, pulling as you go like a drawstring. This creates the closed top of the cactus.

Next, join the short edges of the rectangle together with a whipstitch (see pages 78–79), working through both layers. Now only the bottom of the cactus will be open. Stuff generously with polyfill.

Finally, work the same drawstring closure you used for the top of the cactus along the bottom edge of the cactus, pulling closed as you go.

Once the seams are complete, use the same tail to sew the cactus to the soil, attaching it on all sides, all the way around.

Flowers (make 3)

Using scraps of pink yarn, make a magic circle.

Round 1: 6 sc in the magic circle.

Round 2: Sl st to first sc. *In the same st you did the sl st in* [ch 2, tr, dc], *sl st in next st, *in same st you did the sl st in* [ch 2, tr, dc]; repeat from * around. Sl st in first st to end round.

Fasten off, leaving a short tail for attaching the flower to the cactus.

Once you have completed 3 flowers, use the tails and a tapestry needle to sew them into the top of the cactus. Weave in all yarn tails.

Tip: **Sc blo:**
Insert hook under back loop only of next stitch, then complete sc as usual: yarn over, draw yarn through first loop on hook, yarn over, draw yarn through both loops on hook to complete the sc blo.

Tip: The completed cactus is nearly 6.5″ from top of flowers to the bottom of soil base. The soil has a circumference of about 9″ around the base and is about 3″ high.

Triangle Shawl with Tassels

Skill Level

BEGINNER

Materials

LIGHT 3 — 1 skein (590 yards) for shawl, 20 yards scrap yarn for tassels

Hook: 5 mm/U.S. H-8

Other: Large tassel maker, scissors, tapestry needle

Stitches Used

Chain stitch (ch)
Double crochet (dc)
Single crochet (sc)

Instructions

Ch 3.

Row 1: Skip the first 2 ch, 2 dc, ch 2, 3 sc in last ch st.

Row 2: Ch 2, turn. Dc in same st as ch 2, dc in next 2 sts, (2 dc, ch 2, 2 dc) in ch-2 sp, dc in next 2 sts, 2 dc in last st.

Row 3: Ch 2, turn. Dc in same st as ch 2, dc in each dc st to ch-2 sp, (2 dc, ch 2, 2 dc) in ch-2 sp, dc in each st to last st, 2 dc in last st.

Rows 4–7: Repeat row 3.

Rows 8–12: Ch 2, turn. Dc in same st as ch 2, dc in each dc st to ch-2 sp, (2 dc, ch 2, 2 dc) in ch-2 sp, dc in each st to last st, 2 dc in last st.

Row 13: Ch 2, turn. Dc in same st as ch 2. *Ch 1, skip 1 st, 1 dc; repeat from * to ch-2 sp. Ch 1, (2 dc, ch 2, 2 dc) in ch-2 sp. **Ch 1, skip 1 st, dc; repeat from ** to end of row. Ch 1, skip 1 st, 2 sc in last st.

Rows 14–41: Repeat rows 8–13.

Fasten off and weave in yarn tails.

Tassels (make 2)

The shawl will likely use all 590 yards of yarn, so you'll need additional yarn to make the tassels. Each tassel on this shawl is made with 10-yard scraps of 4/medium yarn, but you can use any yarn weight—just adjust the number of wraps to compensate for thicker or thinner yarn.

Step 1: Adjust large tassel maker to desired height from the front side. Flip to back side of tassel maker and tuck yarn tail into the notch on one side as shown above.

Step 2: Wrap yarn around the tassel maker 15 times; the more wraps, the thicker the tassel. Tuck the end of the yarn into the notch on the other side of the tassel maker.

Step 3: Trim yarn end. Cut 2 lengths of yarn—one about 12″ long, the other about 8″ long.

Step 4: Place the 12″ length of yarn under the vertical wraps of yarn.

Step 5: Tie 2 tight knots in the side facing up—the tighter the better.

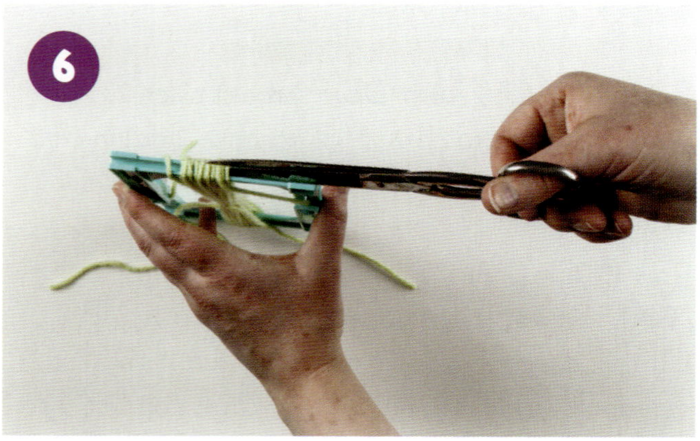

Step 6: Place scissors in the groove at the top of the tassel maker frame and cut wrapped strands of yarn.

Tip: You can also use a piece of cardboard or a book to create your own tassel maker.

Step 7: Turn tassel maker frame over, place scissors in groove, and cut wrapped strands of yarn to remove tassel. Above is the tassel completely removed from the frame.

Step 8: Fold the top half of the tassel down. Pull the 2 long ends from the knots you tied in the middle up to the top. You will use these to attach the tassel to the shawl later.

Step 9: Place the 8″ length of yarn under the top of the tassel as shown. This will form the head.

Step 10: Tie a knot on this side.

Step 11: Wrap the yarn around and tie another knot on the other side.

Step 12: Take tassel in hand as shown here and trim tassel ends to neaten.

Step 13: Find corner of shawl where tassel will be attached. Thread one yarn tail through a tapestry needle.

Step 14: Insert the threaded tapestry needle up through a corner stitch.

Step 15: Draw yarn through. Thread the other yarn tail through a tapestry needle.

Step 16: Insert threaded tapestry needle through another nearby corner stitch (do not use same corner stitch as step 14). Draw yarn through.

Step 17: Tie a double knot with the 2 yarn tails.

Step 18: Insert needle threaded with yarn tail into top of tassel head. Repeat with other yarn tail. Once both yarn tails are through tassel, trim excess yarn.

Mandala Wall Hanging

Skill Level

EASY

Materials

MEDIUM 4 in 3 colors

Hook: 5 mm/U.S. H-8

Other: 8″ embroidery hoop, tapestry needle

Stitches Used

Chain stitch (ch)
Double crochet (dc)
Double crochet increase (dc inc)
Magic circle
Single crochet (sc)
Single crochet increase (sc inc)
Slip stitch (sl st)

Tip: This project doesn't take much yarn and is a great way to use up yarn scraps! This example uses 3 colors: color 1 is white, color 2 is orange, and color 3 is blue.

Instructions

With color 1 (white), make a magic circle.

Round 1: Ch 3, make 11 dc into the magic circle. Sl st in top of ch 3 to complete round.

Change to color 2 (orange).

Round 2: Ch 3, dc inc in each st around. Sl st in top of ch 3 to complete round.

Change to color 3 (blue).

Round 3: Ch 1, *sc, sc inc; repeat from * around. Sl st in top of ch 1 to complete round.

Change to color 2 (orange).

Round 4: Ch 1, *2 sc, sc inc; repeat from * around. Sl st in top of ch 1 to complete round.

Change to color 1 (white).

Round 5: Ch 3, *3 dc, dc inc; repeat from * around. Sl st in top of ch 3 to complete round.

Change to color 3 (blue).

Round 6: Ch 1, *4 sc, sc inc; repeat from * around. Sl st in top of ch 3 to complete round.

Round 7: Ch 3, dc in each st around. Sl st in top of ch 3 to complete round.

Tip: **How to sc increase:**
Work a single crochet into next stitch of previous round, inserting your hook under the top 2 loops of stitch. Work a 2nd single crochet into that same stitch to complete the sc increase.

Tip: **How to dc increase:**
Work a double crochet into the next stitch of previous round, inserting your hook under the top 2 loops of stitch. Work a 2nd double crochet into that same stitch to complete the dc increase.

Attaching the Hoop

Place mandala inside inner embroidery hoop (see picture 1). Unscrew and remove outer embroidery hoop. Set aside for now.

Attach mandala to inner embroidery hoop with a single crochet in each stitch around: Insert hook through hoop and into next stitch (as seen in picture 2). Working under hoop: yarn over and draw through first loop on hook. You will have 2 loops on hook. Working above hoop (as seen in picture 3): yarn over and draw through both loops on hook. You will have 1 loop on hook each time you complete a single crochet (as seen in picture 4).

The first few stitches around the hoop can be tricky but it will become easier as you go. Continue to single crochet in each stitch around, doing your first yarn over and draw through under the hoop, then completing the single crochet over the hoop with the 2nd yarn over. Fasten off and weave in yarn tail. Replace outer embroidery hoop and tighten screw.

Picture 1

Picture 2

Picture 3

Picture 4

Baby Booties

Skill Level

INTERMEDIATE

Materials

150 yards

Hook: 4.5 mm/U.S. 7
Other: 2 buttons, needle, thread

Stitches Used

Chain stitch (ch)
Double crochet (dc)
Double crochet 2 together (dc2tog)
Half double crochet (hdc)
Single crochet (sc)
Single crochet 2 together (sc2tog)
Slip stitch (sl st)

Instructions

0-3 months sizing. (Using a larger hook will create a slightly larger bootie.)

Booties will be worked in continuous rounds.

Ch 9.

Round 1: Work 3 sc in 2nd ch from hook, sc in next 3 ch, hdc in next ch, dc in next 2 ch, 7 dc in last ch. Cont working across opposite side of foundation ch, dc in next 2 ch, hdc in next ch, sc in next 3 ch.

Round 2: Cont around, starting in top of first sc of prev rnd, 2 sc in next 3 sts, sc in next 7 sts, 2 sc in next 5 sts, sc in next 7 sts.

Round 3: [Sc in next st, 2 sc in next st] 3 times, sc in next 7 sts, [sc in next st, 2 sc in next st] 5 times, sc in next 7 sts.

Round 4: Sc all around except last st. Hdc in last st.

Round 5: 8 dc, 1 hdc, 29 sc.

Round 6: Sc2tog once, 6 sc, sc2tog once, 7 sc, sc2tog 7 times, 7 sc.

Round 7: 15 sc, dc2tog 4 times, 6 sc.

Round 8 right bootie: Sl st 12, ch 12, sc in 5th ch from hook, sc down ch and sl st in next st on bootie. Sl st 12. Fasten off and weave in ends.

Round 8 left bootie: Sl st 22, ch 12, sc in 5th ch from hook, sc down ch and sl st in next st on bootie. Sl st 2. Fasten off and weave in ends.

Finishing

Using a needle and thread, sew a small button on each bootie corresponding with the buttonhole on the strap.

Tip: These baby booties make a great keepsake gift for any newborn. Experiment with different types of yarn to make the perfect pair!

Table Centerpiece

Skill Level
INTERMEDIATE

Materials

MEDIUM 4 — 2 skeins, 1 of each color (120 yards per skein)

Hook: 4.5 mm/U.S. 7
Other: Tapestry needle

Stitches Used

Chain stitch (ch)
Double crochet (dc)
Picot stitch
Single crochet (sc)
Single crochet in front loop only (sc flo)
Slip stitch (sl st)

Tip: Work rows 7–9 and 25–27 in the edging color, or a new color, to add a pop of color.

Instructions

Ch 38.

Work all sc sts in front loop only (flo) unless directed otherwise.

Row 1: Sc flo in 3rd ch from hook and in every ch to end of row.

Rows 2–6: Ch 2, turn. Work entire row in sc flo.

Row 7: Ch 3, turn. Dc in next st. Sk next 2 sts. *(Dc, ch 1, dc) in next st, sk 2 sts; rep from * 11 times total. Work 1 more dc in each of the last 2 sts.

Row 8: Ch 3, turn. Dc in next st. Working in ch-1 sps, *(dc, ch 1, dc) in each sp; rep from * 11 times total. Work 2 more dc to end row.

Row 9: Ch 2, turn. Sc flo in first dc st from prev row. Working in the sps from prev row, sc flo in each sp bet dc sts, and 2 sc flo in each ch-1 sp. At the end of the row, sc flo in the last dc and last ch of tch.

Rows 10–24: Ch 2, turn. Work entire row in sc flo.

Row 25: Repeat row 7.

Row 26: Repeat row 8.

Row 27: Repeat row 9.

Edging

Work in back loop only (blo) of sts unless directed otherwise.

Round 1: Ch 2. Work sc sts across the top edge of the work, making sure to space them evenly. (Sc, ch 2, sc) in each corner and cont working around.

Round 2: Ch 2, sc in next sc, ch 1, sk 1 sc, sc in next sc st, *(ch 1, sk next sc, sc in next sc) until end of row, ch 1 (sc, ch 2, sc) in corner sp. Rep from * around, sl st to join in beg of rnd.

Round 3: Ch 3, sk next sc, sc in the sp formed by the ch st in prev row, *(ch 1, sk next sc, sc in sp from prev row), ch 1, (sc, ch 2, sc) in corner sp. Rep from * around, sc in same ch-2 corner sp that last sc was worked. Ch 1, sl st to join work in beg of rnd.

Round 4: Ch 3, sc in sp below, *(ch 1, sk next sc, sc in sp below) until end of row, ch 1 (sc, ch 2, sc) in corner sp. Rep from * around. Sc in same ch-2 corner sp that last sc st was worked. Ch 1, sc, ch 1, sl st to join work in beg of rnd.

Round 5: (Work all dc sts in the ch-1 sps formed in the prev row.) Ch 3, dc, skipping next sc, insert hook in next ch-1 sp, ch 1, dc in same ch-1 sp as prev dc. *(Ch 1, dc skipping next ch-1 sp and inserting hook in following ch-1 sp. Ch 1, dc in same ch-1 sp as prev dc) rep until end, ch 1, dc in ch corner sp, ch 3 to form corner; rep from * around. Dc in same ch-2 corner sp, ch 2, dc in the sl st at the base of the first 3 ch sts that began the rnd. Ch 1, sl st to 3rd ch to join.

Round 6: (Work all sc sts in ch-1 sps from prev row.) Ch 2, *(sc in ch-1 sp, ch 3, sl st in first ch to form picot. Sc in same ch-1 sp, sc in next ch-1 sp); rep from * until end of row, (2 sc, ch 1, dc, ch 1, 2 sc) in corner sp; rep from * around. Sc in next ch-1 sp. Sc in next ch-1 sp bet dc sts. Ch 3, sl st to first ch to form picot, sc in same ch-1 sp. Sl st to join in beg of rnd. Fasten off and weave in ends.

Mug Cozy

Skill Level

EASY

Materials

MEDIUM 4 less than 120 yards

Hook: 4.5 mm/U.S. 7

Other: 1 button, pin, tapestry needle

Stitches Used

Chain stitch (ch)
Double crochet (dc)
Half double crochet (hdc)
Single crochet (sc)
Slip stitch (sl st)

Instructions

Ch 8.

Row 1: 1 sc and 1 dc in 2nd ch from hook, *sk next ch, 1 sc and 1 dc in next ch; repeat from * to end of row, ch 1, turn.

Row 2: *Sk next st, 1 sc and 1 dc in next st; repeat from * to end of row, ch 1, turn.

Rep row 2 until work measures 8″ from beg.

Next row: Sk first st, sl st in the next 2 sts, 1 hdc in each of the next 4 sts, ch 1, turn.

You will now be working on these 4 sts to make buttonhole strip.

Next row: 1 hdc in each st, ch 1, turn.

Rep last row until buttonhole strip measures 2″.

Next row: 1 hdc in first st, ch 2 and sk next 2 sts, 1 hdc in last st.

Work sc border evenly around, working 3 sc in corners and 2 sc in ch-2 buttonhole sp. Join with sl st in first sc.

Finishing

Fasten off and weave in ends.

Attach the button.

Tip: **Attaching the button:**

1. Wrap your cozy around your mug so you can see where you want the button to go. Mark it with a pin.
2. Thread a tapestry needle with a piece of yarn about 7″ long.
3. Place your button where you have marked with a pin. Remove the pin and hold the button in place.
4. Insert the needle from back to front through 1 buttonhole. (Leave about a 2″ tail on the back side.) Insert the needle through the next hole from the front. Repeat until you feel the button is secure.
5. Make a knot with the 2 tails that are left and cut the excess yarn.

Bear

Skill Level

EASY

Materials

MEDIUM 4 380-yard skeins in light brown and cream (you'll have leftover yarn, especially in cream), plus 12″ black scrap yarn

Hook: 4 mm/U.S. G-6

Other: Pins, polyfill stuffing, 10 mm safety eyes, stitch marker, tapestry needle

Stitches Used

Magic circle
Single crochet (sc)
Single crochet 2 together (sc2tog)
Single crochet in front loop only (sc flo)
Single crochet join

Instructions

Use a stitch marker to mark the beginning of each round.

Head and Body

Head and body are worked as one piece, starting with the head. With light brown yarn, make a magic circle.

Round 1: 6 sc in magic circle.

Round 2: 2 sc in each st around.

Round 3: *2 sc in next st, sc in next st; repeat from * around.

Round 4: *2 sc in next st, sc in each of next 2 sts; repeat from * around.

Round 5: *2 sc in next st, sc in each of next 3 sts; repeat from * around.

Round 6: *2 sc in next st, sc in each of next 4 sts; repeat from * around.

Round 7: *2 sc in next st, sc in each of next 5 sts; repeat from * around.

Round 8: *2 sc in next st, sc in each of next 6 sts; repeat from * around.

Round 9: *2 sc in next st, sc in each of next 7 sts; repeat from * around.

Round 10: *2 sc in next st, sc in each of next 8 sts; repeat from * around.

Round 11: *2 sc in next st, sc in each of next 9 sts; repeat from * around.

Rounds 12–25: Sc in each st around.

Round 26: *Sc2tog, sc in each of next 9 sts; repeat from * around.

Round 27: *Sc2tog, sc in each of next 8 sts; repeat from * around.

Round 28: *Sc2tog, sc in each of next 7 sts; repeat from * around.

Round 29: *Sc2tog, sc in each of next 6 sts; repeat from * around.

Round 30: Sc flo in each st around. Add two 10 mm safety eyes between rounds 17 and 18, about 7–8 sts apart. (See pages 65–66 for safety eyes.) Begin stuffing head with polyfill.

Round 31: *2 sc in next st, sc in each of next 6 sts; rep from * around.

Round 32: Sc in each st around.

Round 33: *2 sc in next st, sc in each of next 7 sts; rep from * around.

Round 34: Sc in each st around.

Round 35: *2 sc in next st, sc in each of next 8 sts; rep from * around.

Round 36: Sc in each st around.

Round 37: *2 sc in next st, sc in each of next 9 sts; rep from * around.

Round 38: Sc in each st around.

Round 39: *2 sc in next st, sc in each of next 10 sts; rep from * around.

Rounds 40–52: Sc in each st around.

Round 53: *Sc2tog, sc in each of next 10 sts; rep from * around.

Round 54: *Sc2tog, sc in each of next 9 sts; rep from * around.

Round 55: *Sc2tog, sc in each of next 8 sts; rep from * around.

Round 56: *Sc2tog, sc in each of next 7 sts; rep from * around.

Round 57: *Sc2tog, sc in each of next 6 sts; rep from * around.

Round 58: *Sc2tog, sc in each of next 5 sts; rep from * around.

Round 59: *Sc2tog, sc in each of next 4 sts; rep from * around.

Round 60: *Sc2tog, sc in each of next 3 sts; rep from * around. Stuff body with polyfill.

Round 61: *Sc2tog, sc in each of next 2 sts; rep from * around.

Round 62: *Sc2tog, sc in next st; rep from * around.

Round 63: Sc2tog around. Fasten off, leaving long tail. With tapestry needle and tail, sew bottom closed and weave in end.

Arms (make 2)

With light brown yarn, make a magic circle.

Round 1: 6 sc in magic circle.

Round 2: 2 sc in each st around.

Round 3: *2 sc in next st, sc in next st; repeat from * around.

Round 4: *2 sc in next st, sc in each of next 2 sts; rep from * around.

Round 5: *2 sc in next st, sc in each of next 3 sts; rep from * around.

Rounds 6–8: Sc in each st around.

Round 9: *Sc2tog, sc in each of next 3 sts; repeat from * around.

Rounds 10–21: Sc in each st around. Stuff arm with polyfill.

Single Crochet Join

Step 1: Flatten the arm opening so that stitches line up.

Step 2: Insert your hook from front to back under the first pair of stitches on the right.

Step 3: Yarn over and draw through the loop on your hook. Yarn over and draw through both loops on your hook.

Step 4: With your first single crochet done, insert your hook under the next pair of stitches and work another single crochet.

Step 5: Continue working a single crochet into each pair of stitches across the seam. Fasten off, leaving long tail.

Legs (make 2)

Beginning with cream yarn, make a magic circle.

Round 1: 6 sc in magic circle.

Round 2: 2 sc in each st around.

Round 3: *2 sc in next st, sc in next st; repeat from * around.

Round 4: *2 sc in next st, sc in next 2 sts; repeat from * around.

Round 5: *2 sc in next st; sc in each of next 3 sts; rep from * around.

Round 6: *2 sc in next st; sc in each of next 4 sts; rep from * around.

Round 7: Sc in each st around.

Change to light brown yarn.

Rounds 8–9: With light brown, sc in each st around.

Round 10: *Sc2tog, sc in each of next 4 sts; repeat from * around.

Round 11: *Sc2tog, sc in each of next 3 sts; repeat from * around.

Rounds 12–23: Sc in each st around. Stuff leg and flatten opening so that stitches line up. Sc along opening through both sts to close leg. Fasten off, leaving long tail.

Ears (make 2)

With light brown yarn, make a magic circle.

Round 1: 6 sc in magic circle.

Round 2: 2 sc in each st around.

Round 3: *2 sc in next st, sc in next st; repeat from * around.

Round 4: *2 sc in next st, sc in each of next 2 sts; rep from * around.

Round 5: *2 sc in next st, sc in each of next 3 sts; rep from * around.

Rounds 6–8: Sc in each st around. Flatten ear opening so that stitches line up. Sc along opening through both sts to close ear. Fasten off, leaving a long tail.

Muzzle

With cream yarn, make a magic circle.

Round 1: 6 sc in magic circle.

Round 2: 2 sc in each st around.

Round 3: *2 sc in next st, sc in next st; repeat from * around.

Round 4: *2 sc in next st, sc in each of next 2 sts; rep from * around.

Round 5: *2 sc in next st, sc in each of next 3 sts; rep from * around.

Round 6: *2 sc in next st, sc in each of next 4 sts; rep from * around. Fasten off, leaving long tail.

Making the Nose

Using the strand of black scrap yarn and a tapestry needle, embroider a nose.

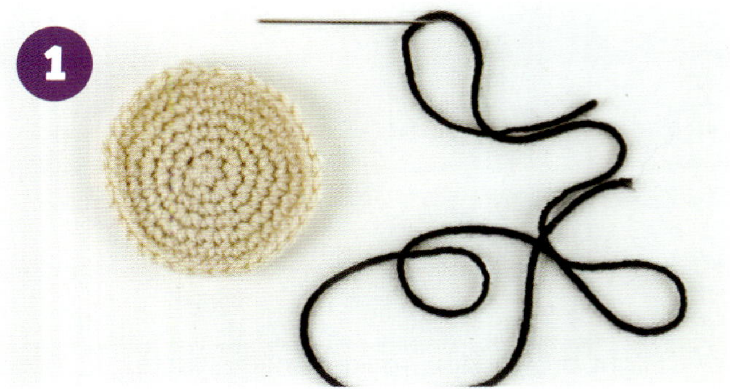

Step 1: Thread a tapestry needle with strand of black scrap yarn.

Step 2: With right (front) side of muzzle facing up, bring needle up from back to front on one side and down from front to back on opposite side.

Step 3: Bring needle up from the same place as before and insert down through opposite side again to create horizontal part of nose.

Step 4: To create triangle shape, make narrower lines across each subsequent row. Bring needle up from below and insert down at tip of triangle.

Step 5: Bring needle up from same place as before and insert down at tip of triangle again to double over part you just did. Trim yarn. You don't need to knot anything on wrong (back) side of muzzle.

Assembly

Using a tapestry needle and yarn tails, assemble bear as follows. Pin each part onto body in desired position before sewing.

1. Sew ears onto either side of head.
2. Sew muzzle onto head under eyes, stuffing lightly with polyfill.
3. Sew on arms and legs: bring threaded needle under loop in body, then through arm or leg. Continue drawing needle through part of body, then part of limb, across seam. Loop knot when done and bring needle out of body far from limb attachment. Trim yarn.
4. Make sure all ends are woven in.

Flower Bookmark

Skill Level

EASY

Materials

MEDIUM 4 less than 15 yards

Hook: 3.5 mm/U.S. E-4
Other: Tapestry needle

Stitches Used

Chain stitch (ch)
Double crochet (dc)
Half double crochet (hdc)
Magic circle
Single crochet (sc)
Slip stitch (sl st)

Instructions

Large Flower

Make a magic circle.

Round 1: 5 sc in magic circle. Sl st in first sc to close the round.

Round 2: Ch 1, sc in same st as initial ch 1, *(ch 4, sc in next st); repeat from * around. Sl st in first sc to close round.

Round 3: *Sl st in ch-4 sp, *working in same ch-4 sp*: (ch 1, 2 dc, hdc, 2 dc, ch 1, sl st); rep from * around. Sl st in first sl st to close round.

Ch 55 for stem. Add or subtract chains for a longer or shorter bookmark.

Small Flower

Sl st in 4th ch from hook to create a ring.

Round 1: *Working into the ring:* *(ch 1, dc, ch 1, sc); rep from * 5 times. Sl st in first ch 1 to close. Fasten off and weave in all yarn tails.

Tip: The finished bookmark is about 14″ long from end to end.

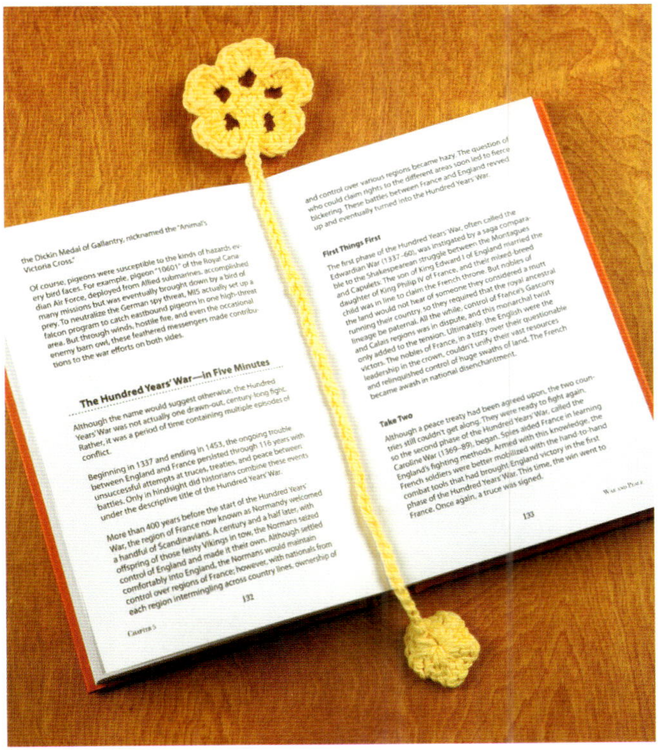

Round Basket

Skill Level

EASY

Materials

MEDIUM 4 — 360 yards of main color, 120 yards of border color

Hook: 5 mm/U.S. H-8

Other: Tapestry needle

Stitches Used

Chain stitch (ch)
Magic circle
Single crochet (sc)
Single crochet in back loop only (sc blo)
Single crochet increase (sc inc)
Single crochet spike stitch (sc spike st)
Slip stitch (sl st)

Instructions

Work entire pattern using 2 strands of yarn held together at the same time, treating the 2 strands as 1 strand.

Using main color (here in tan), make a magic circle.

Round 1: 6 sc in magic circle. Sl st in top of first sc to close round.

Round 2: Ch 1, sc inc in each st around. Sl st in top of first sc to close.

Round 3: Ch 1, *sc, sc inc; rep from * around. Sl st in top of first sc to close.

Round 4: Ch 1, *2 sc, sc inc; rep from * around. Sl st in top of first sc to close.

Round 5: Ch 1, *3 sc, sc inc; rep from * around. Sl st in top of first sc to close.

Round 6: Ch 1, *4 sc, sc inc; rep from * around. Sl st in top of first sc to close.

Round 7: Ch 1, *5 sc, sc inc; rep from * around. Sl st in top of first sc to close.

Round 8: Ch 1, *6 sc, sc inc; rep from * around. Sl st in top of first sc to close.

Round 9: Ch 1, *7 sc, sc inc; rep from * around. Sl st in top of first sc to close.

Round 10: Ch 1, *8 sc, sc inc; rep from * around. Sl st in top of first sc to close.

Round 11: Ch 1, *9 sc, sc inc; rep from * around. Sl st in top of first sc to close.

Round 12: Ch 1, *10 sc, sc inc; rep from * around. Sl st in top of first sc to close.

Round 13: Ch 1, sc in each st around. Sl st in top of first sc to close.

Round 14: Ch 1, sc blo in each st around. Sl st in top of first sc to close.

Rounds 15–28: Ch 1, sc in each st around. Sl st in top of first sc to close.

Tip: The finished basket is about 10″ across and 6″ high.

Change to border color (here in blue).

Round 29: Ch 1, *sc spike st in next st, sc in next st; rep from * around. Sl st in top of first sc to close.

Round 30: Ch 1, *sc spike st in next st, sc in next st; rep from * around. Sl st in top of first sc to close.

Round 31: Repeat round 29.

Round 32: Repeat round 30.

Round 33: Sl st in each st around. Sl st in first sl st to close.

Fasten off and weave in yarn tails.

Tip: **Sc spike stitch:**
Instead of inserting hook under top loops of next stitch, insert hook into space directly below next stitch 1 round down. Yo, draw yarn through stitch. Pull resulting loop up to height of current round. Yo, draw yarn through both loops on hook to complete a sc spike st. Note: Because pattern is worked holding 2 strands of yarn together, each yo and resulting loop on hook will contain 2 strands. Treat each 2-loop set as 1 loop regardless of stitch.

Lacy Scarf

Skill Level

EASY

Materials

SUPER FINE 1 — 3 skeins (approx. 498 yards total)

Hook: 3.5 mm/U.S. E-4

Other: Blocking boards, rustproof T pins, spray bottle of water, tapestry needle

Stitches Used

Chain stitch (ch)
Double crochet (dc)
Single crochet (sc)
Shell stitch

Tip: **How to make the shell stitch:**
Make 5 dc in 1 stitch. The top of each shell is the 3rd dc of the 5-dc shell.

Instructions

Ch 44.

Row 1: Sc in 8th ch from hook. *Ch 5, sk 3 ch, sc; rep from * across row.

Row 2: Ch 6, turn. Sc in ch-5 sp, 5-dc shell in next sc, sc in ch-5 sp. *Ch 5, sc in ch-5 sp, 5-dc shell in next sc, sc in ch-5 sp; rep from * across to last ch-sp and ch 5, sc in last sp.

Row 3: Ch 6, turn. Sc in top of 5-dc shell (3rd or center dc of the shell). *Ch 5, sc in ch-5 sp, ch 5, sc in top of 5-dc shell; rep from * across to last ch-sp and ch 5, sc in last sp.

Row 4: Ch 3, turn. 3 dc in sc, sc in ch-5 sp, ch 5, sc in ch-5 sp. *5-dc shell in next sc, sc in ch-5 sp, ch 5, sc in ch-5 sp; rep from * across to last ch-sp, sc in last sp.

Row 5: Ch 6, turn. Sc in ch-5 sp. *Ch 5, sc in top of 5-dc shell, ch 5, sc in ch-5 sp; rep from * across row, ending with a ch 5, sc in top of ch 3 from row 4.

Repeat rows 2–5 until desired length. Fasten off and weave in yarn tails.

Blocking the Scarf

Blocking goes a long way toward giving your crocheted project a finished, professional look. Blocking helps edges lie flat, makes pieces easier to join, and forces your crocheted project to dry in the proper shape. Blocking this scarf will make stitches look less crumpled and more consistent. It will also make the scarf longer and wider. This completed scarf is about 54″ long and 10″ wide after blocking.

Step 1: Prepare a blocking board long enough for your scarf. You can purchase foam blocking boards like these, which fit together, or use another flat, padded surface such as a piece of Styrofoam or corkboard, an ironing board, or a towel-covered couch.

Step 2: Mist scarf with a spray bottle of water until evenly saturated.

Step 3: Stretch damp scarf into desired shape on foam blocking boards (or other prepared surface) and pin around edges using lots of rustproof T pins. Leave undisturbed until completely dry.

Striped Baby Blanket

Skill Level
EASY

Materials

MEDIUM 4 in 4 colors (370 yards of each)

Hook: 5 mm/U.S. H-8
Other: Tapestry needle

Stitches Used

Chain stitch (ch)
Back post double crochet (BPdc)
Double crochet (dc)
Front post double crochet (FPdc)
Half double crochet (hdc)
Herringbone half double crochet (Hhdc)
Single crochet (sc)

Instructions

Using color 1 (here in white), ch 120.

Row 1: Dc in 4th ch from hook, dc in each ch across row. Ch 2, turn.

Row 2: Dc in same st as ch 2, *FPdc around next st, dc in next st; rep from * across row, ending with a dc in last st. Ch 2, turn.

Row 3: Dc in same st as ch 2, *BPdc around FPdc from previous row, dc in next st; rep from * across row, ending with a dc in last st. Change to color 2 (here in aqua) and fasten off previous color.
Ch 1, turn.

Row 4: Sc in each st across row. Ch 1, turn.

Rows 5–20: Hhdc in each st across row. Ch 1, turn.

Row 21: Sc in each st across row. Change to color 1 (white) and fasten off previous color. Ch 1, turn.

Row 22: Sc in each st across row. Ch 1, turn.

Row 23: Sc in each st across row. Change to color 3 (here in light gray-blue) and fasten off previous color. Ch 1, turn.

Tip: **How to FPdc:**
Yo and insert hook under post of next stitch from the front side. Yo and draw yarn around post. Yo and draw yarn through first 2 loops on hook. Yo and draw yarn through remaining 2 loops on hook to complete the FPdc.

Tip: **How to BPdc:**
Yo and insert hook under post of next stitch from the back side. Yo and draw yarn around post. Yo and draw yarn through first 2 loops on hook. Yo and draw through remaining 2 loops on hook to complete the BPdc.

Tip: **How to Hhdc:**
Yo and insert hook into next stitch. Yo, draw yarn through stitch and next loop on hook. You now have 2 loops on hook. Yo and draw yarn through remaining 2 loops on hook to complete the Hhdc.

Rows 24–41: Hdc in first st, *sk next st, [sc, hdc] in next st; rep from * across until last st, sc in last st. Ch 1, turn.

Row 42: Sc in each st across row. Change to color 1 (white) and fasten off previous color. Ch 1, turn.

Row 43: Sc in each st across row. Ch 1, turn.

Row 44: Sc in each st across row. Change to color 4 (here in dark blue) and fasten off previous color. Ch 1, turn.

Row 45: Sc in each st across row. Ch 1, turn.

Rows 46–61: Hhdc in each st across row. Ch 1, turn.

Row 62: Sc in each st across row. Change to color 1 (white) and fasten off previous color. Ch 1, turn.

Rows 63–64: Sc in each st across row. Ch 1, turn. After row 64, change to color 2 (aqua) and fasten off previous color.

Row 65: Sc in each st across row. Ch 1, turn.

Rows 66–83: Hdc in first st, *sk next st, [sc, hdc] in next st; rep from * across until last st, sc in last st. Ch 1, turn.

Row 84: Sc in each st across row. Change to color 1 (white) and fasten off previous color. Ch 1, turn.

Rows 85–86: Sc in each st across row. Ch 1, turn. After row 86, change to color 3 (light gray-blue) and fasten off previous color.

Row 87: Sc in each st across row. Ch 1, turn.

Rows 88–103: Hhdc in each st across row. Ch 1, turn.

Row 104: Sc in each st across row. Change to color 1 (white) and fasten off previous color. Ch 1, turn.

Rows 105–106: Sc in each st across row. Ch 1, turn. After row 106, change to color 4 (dark blue) and fasten off previous color.

Row 107: Sc in each st across row. Ch 1, turn.

Rows 108–125: Hdc in first st, *sk next st, [sc, hdc] in next st; rep from * across until last st, sc in last st. Ch 1, turn.

Row 126: Sc in each st across row. Change to color 1 (white) and fasten off previous color. Ch 3, turn.

Row 127: Dc in each st across row. Ch 2, turn.

Row 128: Dc in same st as ch 2, *FPdc around next st, dc in next st; rep from * across row, ending with a dc in last st. Ch 2, turn.

Row 129: Dc in same st as ch 2, *BPdc around FPdc from previous row, dc in next st; rep from * across row, ending with a dc in last st. Fasten off and weave in all yarn tails.